KALYAN'A SHAT'ANKU
OR THE
MARRIAGE CEREMONIES
OF THE
HINDUS OF SOUTH INDIA

KALYAN'A SHAT'ANKU

OR THE

MARRIAGE CEREMONIES

OF THE

HINDUS OF SOUTH INDIA,

TOGETHER WITH

A DESCRIPTION OF KARUMANTHARUM

OR THE

FUNERAL CEREMONIES, &C.,

BY THE

REV. J. F. KEARNS,

MISSIONARY OF THE SOCIETY FOR THE PROPAGATION OF THE GOSPEL AT PUTHIAMPUTHUR, TINNEVELLY, SOUTH INDIA.

GYAN

Published by

Gyan Publishing House
5, Ansari Road
Daryaganj, New Delhi-110002
Phone: 011-47034999, 9811692060
E-mail: books@gyanbooks.com

Distribution Network
gyanbooks.com
India, USA, Canada, UK, Australia, France

ISBN : 978-81-212-3661-4 (PB)
First Published, 1868

2nd Impression 2020

Printed at: Gyan Press, Delhi.

Kalyan'a Shat'anku or the Marriage Ceremonies of the Hindus of South India,
Author: Rev. J. F. Kearns

KALYÁN'A SHAṬ'ANKU

OR THE

MARRIAGE CEREMONIES

OF THE

HINDUS OF SOUTH INDIA,

TOGETHER WITH

A DESCRIPTION OF KARÚMÁNTHARUM

OR THE

FUNERAL CEREMONIES, &c.,

BY THE

REV. J. F. KEARNS,

MISSIONARY OF THE SOCIETY FOR THE PROPAGATION OF THE GOSPEL
AT PUTHIAMPUTHUR, TINNEVELLY, SOUTH INDIA.

MADRAS:
HIGGINBOTHAM & CO.,
Law Booksellers and Publishers.
1868.

PREFACE.

THE following account of the Marriage Ceremonies of the Hindus of Southern India was obtained in the following manner. Two, and sometimes three, accounts of the ceremony were obtained from as many respectable intelligent Natives of the several Castes, residing in different places, and wholly unconnected, the one with the other. The accounts so obtained were then compared, and afterwards, one account based upon them was drawn up. This again was submitted to *other* educated Natives for their opinions, and upon the MSS., approved, or corrected by them, the following pages have been compiled. The Marriage Ceremonies of the Brahmins are an exception, as I have indicated in the proper place.

J. F. K.

THE MARRIAGE CEREMONIES OF THE HINDUS OF SOUTHERN INDIA.

INTRODUCTION.

THE Hindus are now divided into many castes, and each caste has some ceremony peculiarly its own. There was a time, when there were no castes, orders, varieties of conditions, or mixtures of castes. (*Vayu Purāna.*) When, and under what circumstances, the people became divided into castes we have no information sufficiently reliable to determine. Manu, the great authority in all matters regarding the Hindu religion and its institutions, believed that, there was no original race of men except the four castes of Brahmans, Kshatriyas, Vaisyas, and the Sudras, the three former constituting the "*twice-born*" and "there is no fifth." (*Manu*, x, 4.) The Rig Veda however speaks of "men of the five classes, the four castes" with the Nishadas. (*Rig Veda*, iii, 53; 15 and 16 *quoted* by *Muir.*) In Manu's time the castes had multiplied, and he accounts for the rise of the inferior castes by the mixture of the four so-called original castes. In the category which he mentions there is one caste, the Nishadas, which he says are the children of a Brahman father and a Sudra mother. The Vishnu Purāna, however, gives a very different account of the origin of this caste. In like manner the mode of their creation is variously stated in the standard Hindu writings. That which appears to have been originally merely a *Mystical Statement* became eventually to be literally interpreted, (*Muir's Sanscrit Texts*) and so we are called upon to believe that " the Brahman was created from the mouth of " Brahma; the Kshatriya from his arms; the Vaisya from " his thighs, and to serve these three castes, the fourth " caste was fashioned, the Sudra sprung from his feet." (*Mahabharata, Santi parva.*) Doubtless the mixture of these castes originated new and inferior ones, but there are weighty reasons for believing that, the people whom the last Âryan immigrants found in the South, then probably broken up into clans, were immigrants of a much earlier period; and weakened, perhaps, by divisions and feuds, submitted to the new *regimé*, and in course of time were quietly formed into castes after the fashion already in vogue in Northern India, (*vide Caldwell's Drav. Gram.*) Each class or caste would naturally have some rite or ceremony peculiarly its own, and at the same time, there would be sameness enough to indicate a common origin.

LAWS RELATING TO MARRIAGE.

THE time when a girl should be *given in* marriage is before she is eight years old—before puberty—the Law censures the delay of the marriage beyond the tenth year (*Manu,* ix, 88, 94.)

If a husband be not provided for her, within three years after she has become *marriageable* she may choose a husband for herself. (*Manu,* ix, 90.)

The parties must be of the same class. (*Manu,* iii, 4.) The wife however must not come within the prohibited degrees, *i. e.,* "She must not be descended from his paternal or maternal ancestors, within the sixth degree, and must be one, who is not known by her family-name to be of the same primitive stock with his father or mother." (*Manu,* iii, 5.) That is, she must not belong to the same *Gotra* or family. Among Brahmins there are forty-nine *Gotras,* said to be descendants of seven Rishis, but more properly eight. To marry a woman belonging to the same *Gotra* was considered incest. (*Max. Muller's Sanscrit Lit.*) Hence, "Thou shalt not give thy daughter to a man of the same *Gotra.*" (*Âpastamba.*) "Marriages take place with persons who have not the same *Pravara,*" *i. e.,* do not invoke the same Rishis (*Âsvolâyana,*) and lastly, "Let a man marry a woman who is free from disease, who has brothers, and who is not the daughter of a man having the same ancestors and belonging to the same *Gotra* as himself." —(*Yâjnavalkya.*)

In seeking a wife, the following ten families are to be studiously avoided. 1, The family which has omitted prescribed acts of religion; 2, the family which has produced no male children; 3, that in which the Veda has not been read; 4, that which has thick hair on the body; 5, that which has been subject to hemorrhoids, 6, to phthisis; 7, to dyspepsia; 8, to epilepsy; 9, to leprosy; 10, to elephantiasis.—(*Manu*, iii, 7.)

Having selected the family, the girl is to be selected, and in doing this, the following are to be avoided. A girl with reddish hair, with a deformed limb, or one troubled with chronic disease, one with no hair, one with too much hair, one immoderately talkative, one with inflamed eyes, one with the name of a constellation, of a tree, river, barbarous nation, mountain, winged creature, snake, slave, or with any name raising an image of terror. (*Manu*, iii, 6, et infra.)

There are eight forms of marriage, viz: The *Brahmá*, *Dévas*, *Rishis*, (or Arsha) and *Prajápatis* which are appropriate for Brahmins, and are based upon disinterested motives; the *Gandharva* and *Rakshases*, which are appropriate for Kshatriyas, and are founded, the former on reciprocal desire, and the latter on conquest; the *Asura*, which is practised by Vaisyas and Sudras, wherein the consent of the party giving away the girl is obtained by a pecuniary consideration; and the *Paisacha* where the marriage may have been effected through fraud practised upon the girl, and which is reprobated for all classes. (*Strange*, vol. I, 42, 43; *Macnaughten*, Junr., I, 59, 60.)

Though each class has its characteristic description

of marriage, there is nothing to bind them to the species appropriate to them. A Brahmin for example may contract an *Asura* marriage, and a Sudra a *Brahmá* one. *(Koollooka Bhut on Menu,* iii, 24.*)*

The binding circumstances essential to the completion of a marriage are gift and acceptance of the girl, and the ceremony termed *Sapthapathi*, or the seven steps. The ceremonial in question accomplishes the marriage. The other ceremonies observed, including sacrifice by fire (*Homam*) are of minor significance. The tying the *Thâli*, or nuptial token, by the bridegroom, round the neck of the bride, is a practice sanctioned by usage, but not prescribed in the Sastras. *(Grooheya Sootrum quoted by Strange.)*

The above matrimonial contract in itself fixes the condition of the parties as married, irrespective of the consummation of the marriage when the female, on reaching maturity, is taken home by the husband. It brings the girl, should her husband die, to the state of widowhood with its attendant consequences, and gives her right of inheritance in her husband's family. (*Strange,* vol. I, 37 ; II, 32, 33.)

The ceremony of the "Seven Steps" is wholly confined to the "twice-born ;" tying the Thâli is the ceremony used by all Sudras in the South, and is considered the only ceremony essential to the validity of a marriage.

MARRIAGE CEREMONIES

OF THE

BRAHMINS.

Abridged from Colebrooke and others.

Having previously performed the obsequies of ancestors as is usual upon any accession of good fortune, the father of the bride sits down to await the bridegroom's arrival, in the apartment prepared for the purpose; and at the time chosen for it, according to the rules of Astrology. The jewels and other presents intended for him are placed there; a cow is tied on the northern side of the apartment; and a stool or cushion, and other furniture for the reception of the guest, are arranged in order. On his approach, the bride's father rises to welcome him, and recites the following prayer, while the bridegroom stands before him: "May she (who supplies oblations for) religious worship, who constantly follows her calf, and who was the milch cow when Yama was (the votary), abound with milk, and fulfil our wishes, year after year."

After the prayer abovementioned has been meditated, the bridegroom sits down on a stool or cushion, which is presented to him. He first recites a text of the *Yajurvéda:* "I step on this for the sake of food and other benefits, on this variously splendid footstool." The bride's father presents to him a cushion made of twenty leaves of *cúsa* grass, holding it up with both hands, and exclaiming, "The cushion! the cushion!

the cushion!" The bridegroom replies, "I accept the cushion," and, taking it, places it on the ground under his feet, while he recites the following prayer: "May those plants over which Sóma presides, and which are variously dispersed on the earth, incessantly grant me happiness while this cushion is placed under my feet." Another is presented to him, which he accepts in the same manner, saying, "May those numerous plants over which Sóma presides, and which are salutary a hundred different ways, incessantly grant me happiness while I sit on this cushion." Instead of these prayers, which are peculiar to the *Brahmins* that use the *Sámavéda*, the following text is commonly recited: "I obscure my rivals, as the sun does other luminaries; I tread on this, as the type of him who injures me."

The bride's father next offers a vessel of water, thrice exclaiming, "Water for ablutions!" The bridegroom declares his acceptance of it, and looks into the vessel, saying, "Generous water! I view thee; return in the form of fertilizing rain from him, from whom thou dost proceed:" that is, from the sun. The bridegroom takes up water in the palms of both hands joined together, and throws it on his left foot, saying, "I wash my left foot, and fix prosperity in this realm:" he also throws water on his other foot, saying, "I wash my right foot, and introduce prosperity into this realm:" and he then throws water on both feet, saying, "I wash first one and then the other, and lastly both feet, that the realm may thrive and intrepidity be gained."

An *arghya* (that is, water, rice, and *dúrvá* grass, in a conch, or in a vessel shaped like one, or rather like a boat) is next presented to the bridegroom in a similar manner, and accepted by him with equal formality. He pours the water on his own head, saying, "Thou art the splendour of food; through thee may I become glorious." This prayer is taken from the *yajush;* but the followers of that Véda use different texts, accepting the *arghya* with this prayer, "Ye are waters (áp); through you may I obtain (áp) all my wishes." And pouring out the water with this text, "I dismiss you to the ocean: return to your source, harmless unto me, most excellent waters! but my beverage is not poured forth."

A vessel of water is then offered by the bride's father, who thrice exclaims, "Take water to be sipped:" the bridegroom accepts it, saying, "Thou art glorious, grant me glory;" or else, "Conduct me to glory, endue me with splendour, render me dear to all people, make me owner of cattle, and preserve me unhurt in all my limbs." The bride's father fills a vessel with honey, curds, and clarified butter; he covers it with another vessel, and presents it to the bridegroom, exclaiming three times, "Take the *mad'huparca.*" The bridegroom accepts it, places it on the ground, and looks into it, saying, "Thou art glorious; may I become so." He tastes the food three times, saying, "Thou art the sustenance of the glorious; thou art the nourishment of the splendid; thou art the food of the fortunate; grant me prosperity." He then silently eats until he be satisfied; and after sipping water, he touches his mouth, and other parts of his body with his hand, saying, "May there be speech in my mouth, breath in my nostrils, sight in my eye-balls, hearing in my ears, strength in my arms, firmness in my thighs: may my limbs and members remain unhurt together with my soul."

Presents suitable to the rank of the parties are then presented to the guests. At the marriage ceremony, too, the bride is formally given by her father to the bridegroom, in this stage of the solemnity according to some rituals, but later according to others. The hospitable rites are then concluded by letting loose the cow at the intercession of the guest. A barber who attends for that purpose, exclaims, "The cow! the cow!" upon which the guest pronounces this text: "Release the cow from the fetters of Varuná. May she subdue my foe: may she destroy the enemies of both him (the host) [and me]. Dismiss the cow, that she may eat grass and drink water." When the cow has been released the guest thus addresses her: "I have earnestly entreated this prudent person, saying, kill not the innocent, harmless cow, who is mother of Rudras, daughter of Vasus, sister of Ádityas, and the source of ambrosia."

While the bridegroom is welcomed with these ceremonies, or more properly before his arrival, the bride bathes during the recital of the following texts: Three vessels of water are severally poured on her head, with three different prayers. 1, "Love! I know thy name. Thou art called an intoxicating beverage. Bring [the bridegroom] happily. For thee was framed the inebriating draught. Fire! thy best origin is here. Through devotion wert thou created. May this oblation be efficacious;" 2, "Damsel! I anoint this thy generative organ with honey, because it is the second mouth of the Creator: by that thou subduest all males though unsubdued; by that thou art lively, and dost hold dominion. May this oblation be efficacious;" 3, "May the primeval ruling sages, who framed the female organ, as a fire that consumeth flesh, and thereby framed a procreating juice, grant the prolific power, that proceeds from the three-horned (bull) and from the sun. May this oblation be efficacious."

After the bridegroom has tasted the *Mad'huparca* presented to him, as abovementioned, the bride's right hand is placed on his, both having been previously rubbed with turmeric or some other auspicious drug. A matron must bind both hands with *cúsa* grass amidst the sound of cheerful music.

The bride's father, bidding the attendant priests begin their acclamations, such as, "happy day! auspicious be it! prosperity attend! blessings!" &c., takes a vessel of water containing *tila* (sesamum Indicum) and cúsa grass, and pours it on the hands of the bride and bridegroom, after uttering the words, "*Om tat sat!*" "God the existent!" and after repeating at full length the names and designations of the bridegroom, the bride, and of himself; and then solemnly declaring, "I give unto thee this damsel adorned with jewels and protected by the lord of creatures." The bridegroom replies, "Well be it!" The bride's father afterwards gives him a piece of gold saying, "I this day give thee this gold, as a fee for the purpose of completing the solemn donation made by me." The bridegroom again says, "Well be it!" and then recites this text: "Who gave *her*?" "to whom did he give *her*? Love (or free consent) gave *her*. To love he gave *her*. Love was the giver. Love was the taker. Love! may this be thine! With love may I enjoy *her!*" The close of the text is thus varied in the *Sámavéda*: "Love has pervaded the ocean. With love I accept *her*. Love! may this be thine."

Being thus affianced, the bride and bridegroom then walk forth, while he thus addresses her: "May the regents of space, may air, the sun, and fire, dispel that anxiety which thou feelest in thy mind, and turn thy heart to me." He proceeds thus, while they look at each other: "Be gentle in thy aspect and loyal to thy husband; be fortunate in cattle, amiable in thy mind, and beautiful in thy person; be mother of valiant sons; be fond of delights; be cheerful and bring prosperity to our bipeds and quadrupeds. First [in a former birth] Sóma received thee; the sun next obtained thee; [in successive transmigrations] the regent of fire was thy third husband; thy fourth is a human being. Sóma gave her to the sun; the sun gave her to the regent of fire; fire gave her to me; with her he has given me wealth and male offspring. May she, a most auspicious cause of prosperity, never desert me," &c. After the donation has been accepted as abovementioned, the bride's father should tie a knot, in the bridegroom's mantle over the presents given with the bride, while the affianced pair are looking at each other. The cow is then released in the manner before described; a libation of water is made; and the bride's father meditates the

Gáyatri, and ties a knot with the skirts of the bride's and bridegroom's mantles, after saying, "Ye must be inseparably united in matters of duty, wealth and love." The bridegroom afterwards clothes the bride with the following ceremonies :—

He goes to the principal apartment of the house, prepares a sacrificial fire in the usual mode, and hallows the implements of sacrifice. A friend of the bridegroom walks round the fire, bearing a jar of water, and stops on the south side of it: another does the same, and places himself on the right hand of the first. The bridegroom then casts four double handfuls of rice, mixed with leaves of *sámi* into a flat basket: near it he places a stone and mullar, after formally touching them, and then entering the house, he causes the bride to be clothed with a new waist-cloth and scarf, while he recites the subjoined prayers: "May those generous women, who spun and wound the thread, and who wove the warp and weft of this cloth, generously clothe thee to old age: long-lived woman! put on this raiment." "Clothe her: invest her with apparel: prolong her life to great age. Mayest thou live a hundred years. As long as thou livest, amiable woman! revere [that is, carefully preserve] beauty and wealth." The first of these prayers is nearly the same with that which is used by the followers of the *Yajush*, when the scarf is put on the bride's shoulder. It is preceded by a different one, which is recited while the waist-cloth is wrapped round her: "Mayest thou reach old age. Put on this raiment. Be lovely. Be chaste: Live a hundred years. Invite [that is, preserve and obtain] beauty, wealth, and male offspring. Damsel! put on this apparel." Afterwards, the following prayer is recited: "May the assembled gods unite our hearts. May the waters unite them. May air unite us. May the creator unite us. May the god of love unite us."

The bride then goes to the western side of the fire and recites the following prayer, while she steps on a mat, made of *Viraná* grass and covered with silk: "May our lord assign me the path by which I may reach the abode of my lord." She sits down on the edge of the mat; and the bridegroom offers six oblations of clarified butter, reciting the following prayers while the bride touches his shoulder with her right hand. 1, "May fire come, first among the gods; may it rescue her offspring from the fetters of death; may Varuná, king [of waters], grant that this woman should never bemoan a calamity befalling her children." 2, "May the domestic perpetual fire guard her; may it render her progeny long-lived; may she never be widowed; may she be mother of surviving children; may she experience the joy of having male offspring." 3, "May heaven protect thy back; may air, and the two sons of As'wini, protect thy thighs; may the sun protect thy children while sucking thy breast; and Vrïhaspati protect them until they wear clothes; and afterwards may the assembled gods protect them." 4, "May no lamentation arise at night in thy abode; may crying women enter other houses than thine; mayest thou never admit sorrow to thy breast; mayest thou prosper in thy husband's house, blest with his survival, and viewing cheerful children." 5, "I lift barrenness, the death of children, sin, and every other evil, as I would lift a chaplet off thy head; and I consign the fetters [of premature death] to thy foes." 6, "May death depart from me, and immortality come; may [Yama] the child of the sun, render me fearless. Death! follow a different path from that by which we proceed, and from that which the gods travel. To thee who seest and who hearest, I call, saying, hurt not our offspring, nor our progenitors, and may this oblation be efficacious." The bridegroom then presents oblations, naming the three worlds, separately and conjointly, and offers either four or five oblations to fire and to the moon. The bride and bridegroom then rise up, and he passes from her left side to her right, and makes her join his hands in a hollow form.

The rice, which had been put into a basket, is then taken up, and the stone is placed before the bride, who treads upon it with the point of her right foot, while the bridegroom recites this prayer: "Ascend this stone; be firm like this stone; distress my foe, and be not subservient to my enemies." The bridegroom then pours a ladleful of clarified butter on her hands; another person gives her the rice, and two other ladlefuls of butter are poured over it. She then separates her hands, and lets fall the rice on the fire, while the following text is recited: "This woman, casting the rice into the fire, says, May my lord be long-lived, may we live a hundred years, and may all my kinsmen prosper: be this oblation efficacious." Afterwards the bridegroom walks round the fire, preceded by the bride, and reciting this text: "The girl goes from her parents, to her husband's abode, having strictly observed abstinence [for three days from factitious salt, &c.] Damsel! by means of thee we repress foes, like a stream of water." The bride again treads on the stone and makes another oblation of rice, while the subjoined prayer is recited: "The damsel has worshipped the generous sun and the regent of fire; may he and the generous sun liberate her and me from this [family]; be this oblation efficacious!" They afterwards walk round the fire as before. Four or five other oblations are made with the same ceremonies and prayers, varying only the title of the sun who is here called *Púshạn*, but was entitled *Aryaman* in the preceding prayer. The bridegroom then pours rice out of the basket into the fire, after pouring one or two ladlefuls of butter on the edge of the basket; with this offering he simply says, "May this oblation to fire be efficacious."

Twelve oblations are made with as many prayers. 1, "May this oblation be efficacious and happily conveyed to that being who is fire in the form of a celestial quirister, who is accompanied by truth, and whose abode is truth; may he cherish our holy knowledge and our valour." 2, "Efficacious be this oblation to those delightful plants, which are the nymphs of that being who is fire in the form of a celestial quirister, who is accompanied by truth, and whose abode is truth." 3 and 4, the foregoing prayers are thus varied: "To that being who is the sun, in the form of a celestial quirister and who consists wholly of the *Sámavéda*." "Those enlivening rays, which are the nymphs of that sun." 5 and 6, "That being who is the moon in the form of a celestial quirister, and who is a ray of the sun, and named *Sushmaná.*" "Those asterisms which are the nymphs of the moon, and are called *Bhécuri.*" 7 and 8, "That being who is air, constantly moving and travelling everywhere." Those waters which are the nymphs of air, and are termed invigorating." 9 and 10, "That being who is the solemn sacrifice in the form of a celestial quirister; who cherishes all beings, and whose pace is elegant." "Those sacrificial fees, which are the nymphs of the solemn sacrifice and are named thanksgivings." 11 and 12, "That being who is mind in the form of a celestial quirister, who is the supreme ruler of creatures, and who is the fabricator of the universe." Those holy strains (*Rĭch* and *Sáman*) who are the nymphs of mind, and are named the means of attaining wishes."

Thirteen oblations are next presented during the recital of as many portions of a single text. "May the supreme ruler of creatures, who is glorious in his victories over [hostile] armies, grant victory to Indra, the regent of rain. All creatures humbly bow to him; for he is terrible: to him are oblations due. May he grant me victory, knowledge, reflection, regard, self-rule, skill, understanding, power, [returns of] the conjunction and opposition of the sun and moon, and holy texts *(Vrĭhat* and *Rat'hantara.)*"

Eighteen oblations are then offered, while as many texts are meditated; they differ only in the name of the deity that is invoked. 1, "May fire, lord of [living] beings, protect me in respect of holiness, valour, and prayer, and in regard to ancient privileges, to this solemn rite, and to this invocation of deities." 2, "May Indra, lord or regent of the eldest (that is, of the best of beings) protect me, &c." 3, "Yama, lord of the earth." 4, "Air, lord of the sky." 5, "The sun, lord of heaven." 6, "The moon, lord of stars." 7, "Vrīhaspati, lord [that is, preceptor] of Brahmá [and other deities.]" 8, "Mitra (the sun), lord of true beings." 9, "Varuná, lord of waters." 10, "The ocean, lord of rivers." 11, "Food, lord of tributary powers." 12, "Sóma (the moon), lord of plants." 13, "Savitrī (the generative sun), lord of pregnant females." 14, "Rudra (Siva), lord of [Deities, that bear the shape of] cattle." 15, "The fabricator of the universe, lord of forms." 16, "Vishnu, lord of mountains." 17, "Winds *(Maruts,)* lords of *(gánas)* sets of divinities." 18, "Fathers, grandfathers, remoter ancestors, more distant progenitors, their parents and grand-sires."

Oblations are afterwards made with prayers corresponding to those which have been already cited from the *Sámavéda.* "1, "May fire come, first among the gods," &c. 2, "May the domestic perpetual fire guard her," &c. 3, "Fire, who dost protect such as perform sacrifices! grant us all blessings in heaven and on earth: grant unto us that various and excellent wealth, which is produced on this earth and in heaven." 4, "O best of luminaries! come, show us an easy path, that our lives may be uninjured. May death depart from me, and immortality come. May the child of the sun render me fearless." 5, "Death! follow a different path," &c.

The bride offers the oblations of rice mixed with leaves of *sámi*, letting fall the offerings on the fire in the manner before mentioned, and with the same prayers, but recited in a reversed order and a little varied. 1, "The damsel has worshipped the generous sun in the form of fire; may that generous sun never separate her from this husband." 2, "This woman casting the rice into fire, says, "May my lord be long-lived; may my kinsmen reach old age." 3, "I cast this rice into the fire, that it may become a cause of thy prosperity: may fire assent to my union with thee."

The next ceremony is the bride's stepping seven steps. It is the most material of all the nuptial rites; for the marriage is complete and irrevocable, as soon as she has taken the seventh step, and not sooner. She is conducted by the bridegroom, and directed by him to step successively into seven circles, while the following texts are uttered: 1, "May Vishnu cause thee to take one step for the sake of obtaining food." 2, "May Vishnu cause thee to take one step for the sake of obtaining strength." 3, "Three steps for the sake of solemn acts of religion," 4, "Four steps for the sake of obtaining happiness," 5, "Five steps for the sake of cattle," 6, "Six steps for the sake of increase of wealth." 7, "Seven steps for the sake of obtaining priests to perform sacrifices." The bridegroom then addresses the bride: "Having completed seven steps be my companion. May I become thy associate. May none interrupt thy association with me. May such as are disposed to promote our happiness, confirm thy association with me." The bridegroom then addresses the spectators: "This woman is auspicious: approach and view her; and having conferred [by your good wishes] auspicious fortune on her, depart to your respective abodes."

Then the bridegroom's friend, who stood near the fire bearing a jar of water, advances to the spot where the seventh step was completed, and pours water on the bridegroom's head, and afterwards on the bride's while a prayer abovementioned is recited: "May waters and all the gods cleanse our hearts; may air do so; may the creator do so; may the divine instructress unite our hearts."

The bridegroom then puts his left hand under the bride's hands, which are joined together in a hollow form, and taking her right hand in his, recites the six following texts: 1, "I take thy hand for the sake of good fortune, that thou mayest become old with me, thy husband: may the generous, mighty, and prolific sun render thee a matron, that I may be a householder." 2, "Be gentle in thy aspect and loyal to thy husband; be fortunate in cattle, amiable in thy mind, and beautiful in thy person; be mother of surviving sons; be assiduous at the [five] sacraments; be cheerful; and bring prosperity to our bipeds and quadrupeds." 3, "May the lord of creatures grant us progeny, even unto old age; may the sun render that progeny conspicuous. Auspicious deities have given thee to me: enter thy husband's abode, and bring health to our bipeds and quadrupeds." 4, "O Indra, who pourest forth rain! render this woman fortunate and the mother of children: grant her ten sons; give her eleven protectors." 5, "Be submissive to thy husband's father, to his mother, to his sisters, and to his brothers." 6, "Give thy heart to my religious duties: may thy mind follow mine; be thou consentient to my speech. May Vrīhaspati unite thee unto me."

According to the ritual, which conforms to the *Sáma-véda*, the bridegroom sits down near the fire with the bride, and finishes this part of the ceremony by making oblations, while he names the three worlds separately and conjointly. The taking of the bride's hand in marriage is thus completed. In the evening of the same day, so soon as the stars appear, the bride sits down on a bull's hide, which must be of a red color, and must be placed with the neck towards the east, and the hair upwards. The bridegroom sits down near her, makes oblations while he names the three worlds as usual, and then makes six oblations with the following prayers, and each time pours the remainder of the clarified butter on the bride's head. 1, "I obviate by this full oblation all ill marks in the lines [of thy hands], in the eyelashes, and in the spots [on thy body]." 2, "I obviate by this full oblation all the ill marks in thy hair; and whatever is sinful in thy looking or in thy crying." 3, "I obviate by this full oblation all that may be sinful in thy temper, in thy speaking, or in thy laughing." 4, "I obviate by this full oblation all the ill marks in thy teeth, and in the dark intervals between them; in thy hands, and in thy feet." 5, "I obviate by this full oblation all the ill marks on thy thighs, on thy privy part, on thy haunches, and on the lineaments of thy figure." 6, "Whatever natural or accidental evil marks were on thy limbs, I have obviated all such marks by these full oblations of clarified butter. May this oblation be efficacious."

The bride and bridegroom rise up; and he shows her, the polar star, reciting the following text: "Heaven is stable; the earth is stable; this universe is stable; these mountains are stable; may this woman be stable in her husband's family." The bride salutes the bridegroom, naming herself and family, and adding a respectful interjection. The bridegroom replies: "Be long-lived and happy." Matrons then pour water, mixed with leaves, upon the bride and bridegroom, out of jars which had been previously placed on an altar prepared for the purpose; and the bridegroom again makes oblations with the names of the worlds, by way of closing this part of the ceremony.

The bridegroom afterwards eats food prepared without factitious salt. During this meal he recites the following prayers: 1, "I bind with the fetters of food thy heart and mind to the gem [of my soul]; I bind them with nourishment, which is the thread of life; I bind them with the knot of truth." 2, "May that heart, which is yours, become my heart; and this heart, which is mine, become thy heart." 3, "Since the food is the bond of life, I bind thee therewith." The remainder of the food must be then given to the bride.

During the three subsequent days the married couple must abstain from factitious salt, live chastely and austerely and sleep on the ground. On the following day, that is, the fourth exclusively, the bridegroom conducts the bride to his own house, on a carriage or any other suitable conveyance. He recites the following text when she ascends the carriage: "O wife of the sun! ascend this vehicle, resembling the beautiful blossoms of the cotton tree and *butea*, tinged with various tints and colored like gold, well-constructed, furnished with good wheels, and the source of ambrosia [that is, of blessings]: bring happiness to thy husband." Proceeding with his bride, he, or some other person for him recites the following text on their coming to a cross road: "May robbers who infest the road remain ignorant [of this journey]; may the married couple, reach a place of security and difficult access, by easy roads; and may foes keep aloof."

Alighting from the carriage, the bridegroom leads the bride into the house, chanting the hymn called *Vámadévya:* Matrons welcome the bride, and make her sit down on a bull's hide of the same color, and placed in the same manner as before. The bridegroom then recites the following prayer: "May kine produce numerous young: may horses and human beings do so: and may the deity sit here, by whose favor sacrifices are accomplished with gifts a thousand fold."

The women then place a young child in the bride's lap; the bridegroom takes up the child, and then prepares a sacrificial fire in the usual manner and makes eight oblations with the following prayers, preceded and followed by the usual oblations to the three worlds. 1, "May there be cheerfulness here." 2, "May thine own [kindred] be kind here." 3, "May there be pleasure here." 4, "Sport thou here." 5, "May there be kindness here with me." 6, "May thine own [kindred] be here benevolent towards me." 7, "May there be delight towards me here." 8, "Be thou here joyous towards me." The bride then salutes her father-in-law and the other relatives of her husband.

Afterwards the bridegroom prepares another sacrificial fire, and sits down with the bride on his right hand. He makes twenty oblations with the following prayers, preceded and followed as usual by oblations to the three worlds. The remainder of each ladleful is thrown into a jar of water, which is afterwards poured on the bride's head. 1, "Fire! expiator of evil! thou dost atone evils for the gods themselves. I, a priest, approach thee: desirous of soliciting thee, to remove any sinful taint in the beauty of this woman." 2, "Air! expiator of evil, &c." 3, "Moon! expiator of evil, &c." 4, "Sun, &c." 5, "Fire, air, moon and sun, expiators of evil! ye do atone evils for the gods. I, a priest, approach thee, desirous of soliciting thee to remove any sinful taint in the beauty of this woman." 6, 7, 8, 9, 10, "Soliciting thee to remove anything in her person which might destroy her husband." 11, 12, 13, 14, 15, "Anything in her person which might make her negligent of cattle."

Multifarious as are the ceremonies connected with a Brahmin's marriage, the only one essential to its validity is the ceremony of the *Seven Steps*; the others are mere non-essential accompaniments, intended to impart solemnity to the ceremony. In the Harrivānsa section of the Maha-bhárata Sátyavrata is charged with the offence of carrying off the wife of one of the citizens; he however denies, that she was the wife of another, because, he says, "the marriage ceremonial is not com-"pleted until the *seventh* step is taken, and *this* had "not been taken when I seized the damsel." *(Muir's Sanscrit Texts.)*

MARRIAGE CEREMONIES
OF THE
VELLALERS.

The first thing which the bridegroom's relations do is to go to the father of the intended bride, and get from him her Sáthagum (Horoscope) which they examine; and the bride's relations examine that of the bridegroom. If both the Sáthagums agree in the eleven essential points, the parties determine upon the marriage and consult an Astrologer for an auspicious day, upon which the bridegroom's nearest relations and friends meet at the bride's house, to arrange for the wedding. A good feast is provided on the occasion, and after the meal, they get a Brahmin, to practice his art, and to foretell, whether they are likely to live a happy and pleasant life.

2. In some part of a room, a large square is formed of chunam; in the south-western corner of which, a brass

lamp is placed, and near it, some cocoanuts are broken, and plantains placed upon one or two plantain leaves.

3. The bride bathes and puts on the cloth brought by the bridegroom's relations, and then, well adorned with flowers and ornaments, she is placed facing the east. The bridegroom's sister brings a basket containing three cocoanuts, three or nine plantains, some areca-nuts and saffron. These presents are divided into three parts, one of which is given to the bride, which she returns to the bridegroom's sister; and the other two, are given to the bride, for her relations and friends. They then settle about the amount of the nuptial present, which when agreed upon, is put into a piece of white cloth, and given to the bride's father, who accepts the offer with great demonstrations of joy.

4. Having received the Brahmin's certificate, the parties purchase the various things required for the wedding feast. The first thing, they buy, is saffron; a quantity of rice is boiled in a new and colored pot, and a cocoanut is broken near the bottom of the pot.

5. Before giving gold to the goldsmith for ornaments, they ascertain "a lucky hour" and "minute," and then take some from the nuptial present, and give it to him to be worked into the required ornaments.

6. On a determined lucky minute, they lay down the first brick in the south-west corner of the place appointed for the *Manavarei*, (a square dais of earth erected in the centre of the pandal) and construct it.

7. A branch from a fig-tree is set up in the south-

west corner of the yard as a *Múhúrtha kâl* (or "marriage post") and then a pandal or shed is constructed.

8. Areca-nuts are first sent to the priest of the temple of Siva and afterwards to all the relations.

9. On the appointed night, a good number of the bride's relations are sent to fetch the bridegroom, who comes in a palkee to the bride's house with great pomp, where he is joyfully received. When approaching the door, some maidens wave their *Alatthi* (lighted camphor) in token of respect; and on entering, he is placed on a cot inside a room. Having partaken of milk and plantain, he comes out again to the *Manavarei* and sits towards the east. A mango stick to which are tied mango leaves, dipped in saffron water, is placed in his hand, which he takes to the south-western corner of the pandal and there plants it. Then he enters another small room to have his face shaven by the barber, who, before commencing his work, worships Piḷḷaiyâr by presenting plantains and cocoanuts. Having shaven, he bathes.

The bride is taken in a palkee to a tank and there she bathes with her maidens, and returns.

10. Now commences the ceremony of "tying the Thâli." A Brahmin seats himself on a part of the *Manavarei*, facing to the north, and before him a bright lamp burns. Beneath this, a Piḷḷaiyâr is made of cow's dung, and by the side of it are placed, a measure of rice, some plantains and cocoanuts.

11. The adorned bridegroom receives sacred ashes from the Brahmin and takes his seat on the other side of the *Manavarei*, facing the east, with his young

friends standing by him. The bridegroom's uncle, (*i. e.*, his *mother's brother*) sits by him and receives his gifts. Afterwards the bridegroom is taken into a room, and the bride is adorned and brought to the Manavarei and seated upon it, facing the east. The bride's *mother's brother* who sits by her, receives his gifts and then retires with her from the Manavarei, into a room.

12. After the bridegroom and the bride have retired to their respective rooms, the new cloths bought for them both, are brought to the Manavârei on two brass trays; and the Brahmin and the other aged men there, bless the cloths and send them into the rooms.

13. At the order of the Brahmin, the adorned bridegroom is brought back to the Manavârei and seated facing the east. The bride is also called for: and being adorned by her maidens, with the new cloth, flowers, and jewels, she is taken into the kitchen where there is a new pot. The bride draws three lines on it with saffron and ties three betel leaves with a little yellow string to its neck. The pot being placed on the fire, the bride pours into it a waterpot full of water and goes to the Manavarei, where she sits at the bridegroom's right side.

14. The bridegroom and the bride, get down from the Manavarei, and make humble obeisance to the assembly, receive sacred ashes from them and go back to their respective places on the Manavarei.

15. The Thâli is put into a little wooden box and brought before the *Guru*, who blesses it himself and

then gives it to the assembly for their blessing. They bless it and return it to the Brahmin.

16. The barber keeps continually blowing the chank. A colored pot is laid on an elephant (either real or earthern); the drums are beaten and the trumpets are blown. The Brahmin pronounces some *Mantras* and gives the Thâli to the bridegroom who slightly ties it round the bride's neck, the bridegroom's sister, however, ties it tightly, and takes off one of the bridegroom's garlands and puts it on the bride's neck. The bridegroom also takes one from his neck himself and puts it on the bride's. The bride then takes one of her's and puts it on the bridegroom's neck.

This is the end of the ceremony of tying the Thâli. The marriage is now complete; but there are the following ceremonies to be gone through also.

17. The Brahmin ties an iron ring and a bit of saffron to both of their hands.

18. The bride's father then says to the bridegroom's father, "I have given my daughter in marriage to your son."

19. The couple then unite their hands and walk round the Manavarei three times, tread upon a grinding stone, look up in the sky at a star and enter the room.

The feast then commences.

MARRIAGE CEREMONIES

OF THE

IDYARS, *i. e.*, THE SHEPHERDS.

The Idyar are so called from *Idai*, the middle, being a kind of intermediate link between the farmers and the merchants. They are divided into eight principal divisions and each of these is subdivided into eighteen branches. Amongst these eighteen, there is only one which associates familiarly with the seventeen above it, the so-called "Branch of the Charitable Works."

2. Determining upon marriage, the dates of the birth of the intended bride and the bridegroom are taken to a Brahmin, who, receiving his fee, casts their Sáthagums (Horoscopes) and names an auspicious day. Or they may go to a temple and while waiting there, should they hear the voice of a lizard, it is considered a good omen.

3. The bridegroom's party go to the Bride's house with presents of a bridal cloth, three cocoanuts, betel, eleven plantains, eleven pieces of saffron and some oil. The latter of these is rubbed on the bride with saffron. Being thus adorned, the bride rides in a palkee and proceeds round the village, worshipping all the gods in her progress, and then starts for the residence of the bridegroom. Having approached the village, the bridegroom's relations go out with butter-milk and jaggery, and invite them to come in. Having received the bride, the bridegroom commences to adorn himself,

and the Brahmin names the hour and minute for the celebration of the marriage.

4. When the bride enters the room with her ornaments upon her, ready for the marriage, her followers pay to the bridegroom's *sister* what is called "Bride's room gold." When the bridegroom sets out for the house of his mother-in-law, he is seized on the way by his young companions and not released until he has paid these a piece of gold. On the third day, when the amusement of sprinkling saffron water on the guests is over, the whole party set out for the tank. The friend of the bridegroom brings a spade and a basket, and the bridegroom fills this basket with earth from the bottom of the tank, which the bride takes up and throws away.

5. The bride and the bridegroom being seated on the Manavarei, and looking towards the east, the Brahmin begins to perform the ceremonies. He makes a ring of grass and puts it on one of the bridegroom's fingers together with an iron ring to keep the devil from touching him. The bride sits at the bridegroom's right.

6. The Brahmin takes the Thâli from a little wooden box, gives it to the old men, for their blessing, and then hands it to the bridegroom, who simply puts it on the bride's neck, but his sister ties it. One of the bride's neck-laces is put on the bridegroom's neck.

7. This is followed by pouring out water to show how much dowry is given to the bridegroom by the bride's parents.—*(See Graul's Reisenach Ostindien.)*

MARRIAGE CEREMONIES
OF THE
MARAVERS.

The Maravers have three different forms of marriages regulated by rank or wealth, &c.

First.—The forms in vogue among the Zemindars of this caste, viz:—

When a young man has made up his mind to marry a girl, a lucky day is determined by the Astrologer, and the parents of the girl are consulted; if all the enquiries are satisfactory, the bridegroom's relations take some plantains and jewels, on an auspicious day, to the bride's house, and there the marriage is agreed upon.

2. After the areca-nuts have been sent to the respective relations, the bridegroom sends to the bride's house in a well-adorned palanquin, a weapon, either a sword, knife or a Maraver's stick, together with some money, betel and the Thâli. The bridegroom's sister puts the weapon, or anything sent to represent the bridegroom, opposite to the bride, and ties the Thâli to her neck in her brother's name.

3. No sooner is this done, than the bride is put in a palanquin and taken to the bridegroom's house where a feast is held for three days, after which, the bride should never be seen outside the house.

4. *Second.*—The ceremonies of the ordinary class of Maravers. They are as follows:—

When the day is settled for the ceremony by a Brahmin, all the relations are invited, who having assembled, the bridegroom and the bride bathe, and are then seated with their ornaments and dress, on the Manavarei, the bride on the bridegroom's left, both facing the east.

5. The Brahmin performs his ceremonies, repeats Mantras to the gods of the winds, fire, clouds, sun and the moon, and invokes them as witnesses to a *bonâ-fide* marriage; and having burned incense to the Thâli, he gives it to the old men of the assembly for their blessing; after which he gives it to the bridegroom's sister who ties it round the bride's neck.

6. The bride's brother lifts her up. A grinding stone with fire upon it in a chatty is also lifted up. The bridegroom walks round the Manavarei three times; the bride follows him, and the stone with the fire is carried after them.

7. Then the bride takes up the pestle of a mortar and holding it as she would a child, carries it round, and her relations give her, each, a sum of money. This is followed by a ceremony performed by the bride's or the bridegroom's uncles, and consists in giving milk and plantain to them.

8. A pot full of saffron water is then produced; into which they put an iron style, and a ring; and the young couple are ordered to take up these from the

pot, and the person who takes the style is said to be the more eminent of the two!

9. *Third.*—Among very poor Maravers, few ceremonies only are performed. They simply have a feast for their relations, place the bridegroom and the bride on the Manavarei, and cause the bridegroom's sister to tie the Thâli; and thus ends the business.

☞ Wives can be taken only from the relations of the *bridegroom's mother;* and never from the father's relations. Strangers are preferable to the father's relations.

MARRIAGE CEREMONIES

OF THE

KURAVERS.

Each party endeavours to ascertain the mind of the other privately; and having ascertained it they consult a Brahmin about the intended marriage. If he gives a favorable answer, the bridegroom's party proceed to the bride's house to arrange for the marriage. They take arrack with them and give it to the bride's father. He also procures arrack, and both parties drink freely of it, distribute betel and then begin to settle the conditions of marriage! The bridegroom's father asks the bride's father, in the presence of several others, whether he intends to give his daughter in marriage to his son. If he replies in the affirmative, the bridegroom's father gives him a little arrack in a

4

cocoanut shell and a piece of tobacco. This is called "the arrack and tobacco of confirmation!" Also a jembú full of water is placed before the couple and a grass named *Thurvi (i. e., Agrostis linearis)* is put into the water. This is equal to an oath between the couple.

2. A feast then follows with arrack and toddy. They again meet after dinner to settle about *Parisam*,* which, if the bride be related to the bridegroom, is four *Narungus*. One *Narungu* is equal to Rupees 8-5-4. Of these four, one is paid immediately, together with Rupees 1-3-4 which is spent in feasting. The other three Narungus are paid at the rate of one per annum!

But if the bride be not related to the bridegroom, the Parisam amounts to ten or twelve Narungus; out of which, four are paid immediately, together with Rupees 1-3-4 for the feast, and the remainder is paid within five years. If these sums are not paid regularly, the bride should be sent away to her father's house!

3. In cases where separation occurs, the sum given as the nuptial present should be returned, and any one willing to pay the same amount may take her again in marriage.

4. On the "Muhûrtham" or marriage day; a pandal is constructed in the bride's house. The bridegroom shaves himself, bathes, and is dressed with new cloths.

* Nuptial present.

Having partaken of some arrack, the bridegroom starts for the bride's house with garlands on his neck, attended by his relations and friends. The bridegroom's sister then goes to the room where the bride is, dresses her with a new cloth, puts garlands on her neck and ties the *Thâli,* and the couple is thereby married.

5. The bride and the bridegroom sit under the pandal facing the east, on a piece of timber covered with a clean cloth. The bride's father takes the right hand of his daughter and places it in the right hand of the bridegroom who holds it. Then they both stand up holding each other's hands, and having walked round the Manavarei three times, retire to a room where they are seated looking eastwards. Then follows a feast of arrack. The next morning the bridegroom and the bride with their relations and friends start for the bridegroom's house.

6. In this caste, children are espoused, even before their birth. Two men who wish to have marriages between their children say one to the other, "If your wife should have a girl and mine a boy, or *vice versâ,* they must marry." And to bind themselves to this, they exchange tobacco, and the bridegroom's father makes a feast of arrack or toddy to the coming bride's relations. But if after the children are grown up, the Brahmin should pronounce the omens unpropitious, the marriage is not consummated, and the bride's father pays back the cost of arrack and other spirits used at the betrothal.

MARRIAGE CEREMONIES

OF THE

SHANARS.

The bridegroom's relations first go to the parents of the intended bride and mention their wishes.

2. On an appointed day, the same persons again go to the house of the bride with a certain sum of money called Parisam (nuptial present) which they give to the bride's father, tied in a piece of cloth, dipped in saffron water. They also settle the amount of jewels the bride shall have, and the value of the earrings that the bridegroom shall put on. At the same time the dowry is settled upon, *i. e.*, what amount of money, or land, or cattle, or vessels of copper or silver shall be given to the bridegroom by the bride's parents.

3. On the day before the marriage, a post is fixed in the front yard of the bridegroom's house, which post is either a thick stick of some milk-tree, (*i. e.*, banian tree, fig tree, &c.,) or a palmyra timber, both newly cut on purpose; and over this, a pandal is constructed which is lined with clean cloths. A square dais of earth is also constructed in the centre of the pandal, and this is called the Manavarei.

4. On the night before the wedding, the bridegroom having shaved his face and bathed with oil is adorned with his best ornaments and best dress.

5. A bamboo stick or a branch of a fig tree is well washed, and garlands are put upon it. This stick is planted in the south-west corner of the pandal, and beneath it is placed a little Piḷḷaiyâr of clay, and a measure of paddy with a lamp upon it. Cocoanuts are broken near it, and betel is offered to it.

6. The barber is sent to fetch another stick of the fig tree to which are tied some bunches of fig leaves. This stick is fixed in the centre of the yard, and called "*Arasanie*" ("the fig stick"); three cups full of cotton seed, and a measure of rice is laid at the bottom of the Arasanie with a Piḷḷaiyâr of cow-dung, and three cocoanuts and three baskets of betel are offered.

7. The uncle richly dressed, is now seated on the Manavarei facing eastward; and a Brahmin or a Guru takes a handful of rice and a few of the leaves from the Arasanie, brings his hand round the uncle's head, and throws them toward the points of the compass. He next takes his seat on a stool facing northward and a present of twenty-one measures of rice and five cocoanuts are given him, with a first-rate pair of cloths.

8. The bridegroom now takes his seat on the Manavarei facing the east, and the Guru takes a handful of rice and a few of the fig leaves, brings his hand three times round the bridegroom's head, and then throws them off towards the four points of the compass.

9. The bridegroom then stands up and walks round the Manavarei, makes obeisance to his uncle by touching his feet, receives the Thâli and the costly cloth for

the bride from him, and resumes his seat on the Manavarei.

10. A potful of water is placed by his side, and garlands are hung upon his neck. The brothers and the nearest relations of the bridegroom come one by one, stoop over the Manavarei facing the west, pick up a few leaves of the fig tree, bring them three times round the bridegroom's head and then throw them into the water. Every member of the family does this.

11. The bridegroom being taken into a room, the Thâli and the cloth for the bride are received from him, and the former placed in a colored little box which is given in charge of the bridegroom's sister, together with the bridal cloth. Betel is now served out.

12. The bridegroom seated in a well-adorned palkee, first goes round the village, breaking several cocoanuts to the gods, and then sets out for the residence of the bride, with several of his relations and others attending him, the drums beating, trumpets blowing, and torches burning. This always takes place at night-time.

13. When the loud blast of trumpets announces the arrival of the bridegroom close to the house of the bride, the bride's relations come out with a good supply of garlands, sandal-wood powder and other kinds of odoriferous stuffs, together with some baskets full of betel. The bridegroom is placed in some house of the bride's relations or in any hired house, where he receives a little food from the bride's parents, who

also serve out the things that they brought to the by-standers and the palkee-bearers.

14. The bridegroom's sister, placed in her brother's palkee, is taken to the bride's house, where she puts oil on the bride's head, who is seated on a colored mat facing the east, combs her hair, and sings some adulatory verses. This done, she receives betel and goes back to the house where the bridegroom is.

15. The bride is taken in the bridegroom's palkee to a tank or a well, her mother's brother or any other uncle sits opposite her in the palkee, the bride reclining on his bosom. They go to the water with a good supply of torches; and there the bride bathes behind a screen of cloth held by the women. She is adorned with flowers and odours, and returns home in the same palkee. On the way, cocoanuts are broken to the gods.

16. The bridegroom now proceeds to the bride's house, with drums, trumpets, torches and the accompanying crowd. When close to the door of the bride, the bride's sisters and near cousins bring a light composed of burning cotton seed, floating in ghee, and this they wave near the face of the bridegroom who then distributes money to them.

17. The bridegroom enters the house of the bride and is seated on the Manavarei with the bride on his left. The Guru or the Brahmin performs his religious ceremonies and Mantras by the side of the Manavarei and receiving the Thâli, blesses it himself first and then gives it to some old man present, to be blessed by him, and afterwards hands it over to the bridegroom.

18. The bridegroom's sister puts the bridal dress on the bride ; and after this, the bridegroom places the Thâli on the bride's neck, which his sister receiving from his hand, ties. This is called '*the holy tie.*'

19. The bride is again seated on the bridegroom's left, and her father places her right hand in the bridegroom's left, who holds it. The two hands are then tied together with a cloth, and they both walk round the Manavarei three times. They are then taken to some other part of the pandal and seated facing the east.

20. The bride's father brings a dish of cocoanut milk and plantain and gives it to the bridegroom. He then unties the cloth from their hands. The garlands are then taken off the bridegroom's neck and put on the bride's.

21. One and the same cloth is put on them both ; and three cups of oil are brought : the bridegroom touches the oil and puts his hand on the bride's head three times ; and the bride does the same to the bridegroom three times. The bride's brother rubs oil on the bridegroom, and his sister on the bride, and then they bathe. This is called the "*shyless bath.*"

22. The bride and the bridegroom make obeisance to their respective relations, who give them money.

23. Next evening, after supper, the bride and the bridegroom are placed in one palkee and brought round the village with great pomp ; drums beating, trumpets blowing and torches burning. Several of the relations also have palkees to ride in. After the procession, when

the couple are brought home, they dispel the supposed effects of the evil-eye, by waving a vessel containing a mixture of chunam, rice, cotton seed and saffron, which is brought round the head of the couple and thrown towards the four points of the compass.

24. The couple are then placed on the Manavarei. The bridegroom holds the bride's right hand with his right, and a pot is laid beneath. The bride's father gets a jembú of water, repeats all the promises of dowry one by one, and pours water over the connected hands, which water falls into the pot below. This is called "*pouring out the dowry.*"

25. On the third day, the bridegroom with his relations, and the bride with her relations, all go to the bridegroom's house, and enjoy a feast. On the fourth day, they all return to the bride's and again feast, when they all bathe with oil. On the sixth, they go back to the bridegroom's house. On the seventh, they return to the bride's. On this occasion, the bride's relations sprinkle saffron water on the bridegroom's relations. On the seventh night, the couple take up their abode in the bridegroom's house.

MARRIAGE CEREMONIES
OF THE
PULLARS.

There are several classes among this caste, but their ceremonies differ only slightly, and there are many, common to all. Both parties refer the matter to a

Brahmin; and if he satisfies them that the fates are propitious, they accordingly make arrangements. The chief men of the village however, sometimes demand a document from them, to the effect that their intentions are *bonâ-fide.*

2. They have several methods of seeking good omens:

(a.) A measure of water is brought to the Guru, who pours melted lead into the water. If the lead runs out branched, this is a good omen. If it only runs in a single bar, this is called a bad omen. Several branches indicate several children.

(b.) Two or three new pots are placed in a room; in one of which is placed a lighted lamp covered. They send a little boy to fetch one of them. If he brings the one with the lamp in it, it is called a good omen.

(c.) A measure is placed half-full of *cholum,* into which a *louse* is put, and then the measure is filled with paddy to its brim; on which is laid a golden jewel, a bit of saffron, and a bit of charcoal, and then they wait for results. If the louse comes up and rests upon the charcoal, it is a bad omen; but good, if it rests on any of the others.

(d.) The mother takes some white oleander flowers and some of the red oleander flowers and ties them in different pieces of cloths. If the white one be brought to her, she calls it a good omen; but if the red one be brought, it is a bad omen: because red denotes blood, and blood denotes death.

3. The chief man of the village, who is called

Kudumban, receives some cocoanuts, plantains and betel in the name of the entire people.

4. The bridegroom's relations go to the bride's house and settle the day for the marriage and give them the Parisam. Having boiled a potful of paddy at a lucky time, a branch of the fig-tree is set up in the south-west corner, as the *Múhúrtha kâl,* amid cheers, or a long roll from the drums.

5. The bride is the first to pound the boiled paddy in a mortar; and the chief persons of the family clean it and prepare the rice.

6. On the appointed day the bridegroom sets out with some show of parade on a pony, for the residence of the bride; and when he reaches it, the bride's sisters wave their *Alatthi* and receive their remuneration, and the bridegroom then seats himself on the Manavarei.

7. The bride goes out in a bandy to some water and there bathes. When she returns, she is adorned with flowers and placed on the bridegroom's left.

8. The bridegroom's sister ties the Thâli round the bride's neck, and then the bride's father or brother gives her hand to the bridegroom, and the bride's uncle or sister-in-law takes her round the Manavarei three times.

9. The couple then proceed round the village; cocoanuts are broken at every altar by way of worship. After coming home, a fowl is brought, one of whose talons they cut and put some of the blood on the forehead of the young couple to "avert the evil-eye," and the fowl is then given to the barber. When all the marriage cere-

monies are over, one or two measures of salt are put into a pot and mixed with water. Two or three rings are put into the water. The bridegroom and the bride are ordered at the same moment to take them from the pot. If the bridegroom recovers them first, he is said to be superior to his wife; but if the bride first recovers them she is said to be the superior: (that is, the husband will in future be submisive to his wife, or *vice versâ.*)

MARRIAGE CEREMONIES
OF THE
PARIARS.

When both parties agree to a marriage they consult an Astrologer, generally a Brahmin, from whom they ascertain a lucky day.

2. On the appointed day for giving the Parisam, the bridegroom with his relations set out for the residence of the bride with as much pomp as possible, taking with them a small cup of oil, some powdered saffron, two or three cocoanuts, seven measures of rice, and the Parisam which the bride's parents agreed to receive. The bridegroom's sister carries these to the bride's house, where she is gladly received. On this occasion they determine the day for celebrating the marriage.

3. Before constructing the pandal, a stick of any green tree is stuck in the ground, and is called the *Máhúrtha kâl.* This post is raised by the headman of the village.

4. The post is colored with saffron in seven places, and seven leaves of betel are tied to it by a thread made yellow with saffron. A measure of rice is placed before the post, and on the rice is laid a little of the grass named *Thurvi*, upon which a Piḷḷaiyâr made of cow-dung is placed. They break cocoanuts and offer incense before the Piḷḷaiyâr.

5. The Manavarei is erected in the centre of the pandal and the relations are all called in. Before they take their meal, uncooked rice is sent to all the chief men of the village, whom they consider their superiors, together with some curry-stuff.

6. Twenty-one pots with their covers are placed upon the Manavarei, upon which the bridegroom's uncle is seated. The bridegroom wears a string like the Brahmins over his shoulder; and then with his uncle touches one of the pots, walks round the Manavarei, touches the second and walks round again. This they do twenty-one times. While they walk round, the drums are beaten, and a man runs to a fig tree, and cuts a branch which is placed in the south-west corner of the pandal. Three cocoanuts are broken while planting the branch.

7. The bridegroom is now adorned with earrings and costly cloths; his parents put garlands over his neck. He rides on a pony round the village with tom-toms preceding him. The bride's father or brother, no sooner hears the drums beating, than he comes out with betel, sandal and garlands; the latter he puts on the

5

bridegroom's neck, and the others are served out to the crowd.

8. The bridegroom is conducted to some neighbour's house until the bride is adorned with flowers, jewels and saffron. She is dressed like a Brahmin woman, with a string such as Brahmins wear, round her. The bridegroom's sister puts upon her the bridal dress after bathing her with oil and saffron.

9. The bridegroom starts for the bride's house, and when he approaches the door, the bride's sisters bring vessels with oil, having cotton seed tied in a rag in the lamp which they burn and wave towards the bridegroom; and for every time they wave it, the bridegroom's father or brother throws them some money. This is called *Alatthi*.

10. The bridegroom is taken to the Manavarei and seated facing the east. The bride's uncle holds the bride's hand and conducts her round the bridegroom on the Manavarei three times and places her at last, seated on his left.

11. At the sound of trumpets, the bridegroom takes the Thâli and ties it slightly round her neck, but his sister ties it tightly. The bride's father or brother gives the bride's right hand into the bridegroom's left; and some sing a few songs in praise of them.

12. The bridegroom's brothers or near cousins get a potful of water, into which fig leaves have been put, some of which they take and bring round the heads of the couple and then throw them behind them.

13. Before the bridegroom lets go his hold of the bride's hand, everything regarding the dowry is settled; and the uncle is presented with a new cloth which they first put on the bridegroom and lift him up three times.

14. Next morning the bridegroom goes to some tank or well outside the village, to bathe, &c.; and he returns, riding a pony with garlands on his neck, and drums and music accompanying him.

15. The oil-bath in the evening at about half past three, is the same as that in vogue with the Shanars, called the "Shyless bath."

16. On the third morning after breakfast, the couple go in procession, the bride's brothers and sisters pelting the bridegroom's relations with cotton seed, the bridegroom and his relations pelting the bride's. On retiring to the bridegroom's house, the bride's relations should take with them twenty measures of rice and thirty small cakes.

After this the bridegroom with a few of his relations tarry in the bride's house a day or two; and when he returns home, some measures of rice and 150 cakes are given him.

MARRIAGE CEREMONIES
OF THE
VANNARS OR THE WASHERMEN.

When a marriage has been determined upon, an Astrologer is consulted, and he having named a lucky day, they determine upon a visit to the bride's house, upon which occasion the bridegroom's party takes with them from four to six measures of rice. Two or three chief men of the village assemble and consult with them with reference to the intended marriage. If there are no objections to it, both parties then name a day on which the bridegroom's relations shall give the Parisam.

2. On the day fixed upon, the bridegroom's relations take with them six and a quarter Rupees, eleven measures of rice, one cocoanut, a cup of oil, seven pieces of saffron and twenty-one betel leaves tied together in *threes.* The bride's uncle being present, receives one Rupee from the Parisam ; and then a day is named for celebrating the marriage.

3. They construct a Manavarei under the pandal, and send areca-nuts to their relations, at the rate of twenty-five to each, but a hundred to the Mûpan or their headman.

4. On the day of the marriage, a certain number of men go to the bride's house to fetch her, pay three fanams (equal to ten annas) and give betel in discharge of what they call " Village money." They then set out

with the bride and place her somewhere outside the bridegroom's village, and some men of the bridegroom's relations take betel with them for the bride's men, bring them home and place the bride in a room. In the south-west corner of the pandal is fixed a branch of a fig tree called the *Kánnikâl*, (" virgin post") and they tie round it fig leaves and bits of saffron.

5. The bridegroom then bathes and goes out with his young men to a temple where he breaks cocoanuts, &c., and returns. Then the bride bathes and goes through the same ceremonies. Another post is then fixed near the Manavarei at an auspicious moment and is called *Nâlkâl* (" the day post") to which is tied some betel leaves, bits of saffron and an iron ring.

6. The Mûpan calls for the Thâli, which is brought in a basket with seven measures of rice, garlands, the bridal cloth and the new cloth for the bridegroom ; the *Mûpan* blesses the Thâli and the bridal cloth and returns them to the bridegroom.

7. The bridegroom gives them to the bride's mother's brother's daughter, who dresses the bride (while the bridegroom is being adorned in the pandal) and then takes her into a room and ties the Thâli herself to the bride's neck, and there ends the *marriage* ceremonies.

8. The bridegroom's friends mark his forehead with three or four lines of black and red dots. His uncle ties some money to one corner of his handkerchief, some others of his relations do the same. With all his orna-

ments and garlands he parades the street, breaking cocoanuts to his gods; and when approaching the door, the bride's sisters to avert the effects of the evil eye, wave the Alatthi.

9. The bridegroom sits on the Manavarei, while the bride is carried by her uncle three times round him, and at last placed at his right side. A cup of milk and a jembú full of water is placed on the Manavarei, and the bridegroom's relations dip a few of the fig leaves first into the water and then into the milk, carry them round his head and throw them at his back. The bride's relations do the same to her.

10. The couple unite their hands, walk round the Manavarei three times, and then go into a room where there are three new colored pots, which they both hold together and take to the kitchen; and there they both boil rice and serve it out afterwards.

MARRIAGE CEREMONIES

OF THE

KULUVARS.

A girl is espoused to a young man befòre she becomes marriageable. On the day of the espousal, a person is sent to fetch all the other Kuluvars, wherever their huts may be; and in their presence the espousal is settled, and the bridegroom gives them a feast of a fat pig and several bottles of arrack.

2. After this, the espoused girl remains in her father's house until she has attained the age of puberty, or until the bridegroom is in a condition to provide for her.

3. On the day of the marriage, the bridegroom should give his father-in-law three pigs of the value of 3½ Rupees each; or if he cannot afford to give these, three fowls or a dog should be given as Parisam.

4. Two pigs are killed for the feast. The young couple are seated upon a pestle inside a screen of cloth, holding each other by their little fingers. The parents of the couple mark their heads and foreheads with a mixture of pounded saffron, cotton seed, chunam and rice.

5. The bridegroom ties a little silver piece of the value of eight or twelve Annas round the bride's neck; two new colored pots filled with water are placed before them, and a brass ring is put in each of them. The couple are ordered to take them from out of the pots and the one who first takes up a ring is reckoned the cleverer of the two.

6. The bridegroom takes hold of the bride's little finger with his little finger, and leads her to his hut and gives his relations three fanams as a present; thus ends the ceremony.

MARRIAGE CEREMONIES

OF THE

KAMMALERS, *i. e.*, THE SMITHS AND CARPENTERS, &c.

The bridegroom's party first go to the bride's parents or guardians and ask their consent to the proposed union. If they consent, a day is fixed on which the relations of the bridegroom go to the bride's house when all her relations are present, with cocoanuts, plantains, a cloth for the bride, betel, saffron and other odoriferous stuffs. On the same occasion the amount of Parisam is settled.

2. The bride bathes and is adorned with flowers, saffron, &c., and puts on the new cloth brought for her; she receives the articles which the bridegroom's party had brought, and gives them to the bridegroom's sisters or cousins.

3. On the auspicious day appointed for the marriage, the relations of the bride go to the bridegroom's house and fetch him in a bandy or palkee to the bride's. Then the Brahmin is sent for, who performs his ceremonies near the Manavarei, the bride and the bridegroom being seated upon it. After the recital of Mantras before the young couple, he sends for their uncles and blesses them.

4. The bridegroom then ties a pilgrim's cloth upon him, places a brass water-pot on his head, holds a torn

umbrella in his hand, and starts out from the pandal and says he is going a sacred journey to Cási (Benárés); when the bride's father runs after him and promises that he *will* give his daughter in marriage to him and swears three times to this effect. The bridegroom being satisfied with this promise, abandons his pretended journey, takes off his pilgrim cloths and gives them with the umbrella to the Brahmin.

5. The couple being now seated on the Manavarei, the Brahmin repeats some Mantras and gives a Brahmin string (Púnúl) to the bridegroom to place over his shoulders. He then blesses the Thâli and hands it to the bridegroom who ties it round the bride's neck, his sister seeing that it is tied properly. The bride's father comes forward and places his daughter's right hand in the bridegroom's right and pours water on them. With their hands united they enter a room where the bridegroom receives from his father-in-law a present of a gold ring.

6. The young couple bathe in oil, which is rubbed by their brother and sister alternately. They then partake of a feast prepared for them and the whole assembly.

7. The Manavarei is now cleansed with cow-dung and ornamented with white and red lines; near it the bride cooks rice in a colored new pot; by the side of her is a Piḷḷaiyâr; near which are, a burning lamp, a measure of rice, cocoanuts, plantains, &c. These fruits and the cooked rice are given to the washerman, and the marriage ceremony is ended.

N. B.—The similarity of some of the Kammáler ceremonies with those of the Brahmins is striking; the use of the Púnúl by this caste, together with the title Achārja, is also interesting.

MARRIAGE CEREMONIES

OF THE

NAICKERS.

The rule with this caste is that the men shall marry the daughters of their sisters, *i. e.*, their neices. Marriages are consequently made by persons between whom there exists a strange disparity of age. Oftentimes the bride is a mere infant, while the bridegroom is a full-grown man and *vice versâ*. There is therefore no need to consult an Astrologer in choosing a wife, but they do consult him in order to ascertain a lucky day for the wedding.

2. On the day named by him, the bridegroom's relations take with them a new cloth for the bride, a string of glass beads, the Parisam, betel, saffron, sandalwood powder and flowers to the bride's house, either walking or in bandies.

3. There, they have a grand feast. This being over, the bride is directed to bathe, and afterwards she is taken to a room where they adorn her with flowers, saffron and sandalwood powder, tie the string of beads round her neck and put on the new cloth which the bridegroom's relations had brought. They then serve

out betel to the whole assembly; this they call "*the betel of confirmation.*"

4. Half the marriage is solemnized, they say, on this day. The amount of Parisam given by the bridegroom's father is now placed in a palkee, adorned with flowers and odoriferous stuffs; carried round the village and brought back. The bride's father takes the Parisam.

5. Both parties prepare the several articles requisite for the wedding: on a lucky minute they begin to boil the first pot of paddy in order to make rice. The Múhúrtha kâl is raised, and areca-nuts are sent to all the relations. A pandal is made and the Manavarei constructed under it.

6. On the auspicious day for the wedding, several of the bridegoom's freinds and relations go to the bride's house to conduct her to the bridegroom's. The bride is adorned with costly ornaments, dress and flowers, taken round the village in a palkee in solemn procession and brought to the bridegroom's house. A loud sound of drums and trumpets announces her arrival. A place is chosen contiguous to the dwelling-place, which is fenced round precisely in the same manner as a fold or pen for cattle: the fence is high and strong; within it a temporary shed is erected, in which the Naicker and his bride are married, "in order to remind them that their fathers were without dwelling-places, tending their flocks in the fields."* A pole is then erected, and

* See the "Tribes of South India, p. 40."

upon it a few branches of the Margosa tree (Melia azidarachta) is tied, by the side of which the bridegroom stands. Some of his female relatives approach, and dipping their forefinger in milk or oil, touch his forehead, shoulders and chest, after which a portion of rice is tossed over his head; he is then seized by a finger and led into the house.

They next procure ten or fifteen earthen pots, which are ornamented with lines drawn by parti-colored chalk upon the outer surface, and place them in a convenient place, one over the other, the females of the house meanwhile chanting in Telúgú.

7. At the directions of the Guru the bridegroom retires to a room to adorn himself. The barber having previously cleansed it with cow-dung, forms a Piḷḷaiyâr and placing it in a corner, offers it a measure of rice, plantains, cocoanuts and betel. After performing these ceremonies, he shaves the bridegroom's face and body and washes him thoroughly, with the exception of the feet, the toe nails of which are cut in the presence of the bridegroom's relations. The barber brings a cup of milk, with which he washes the feet and then he cuts the nails. The milk which remains he carries round to the assembled guests, many of whom throw money into it.

8. The carpenter prepares a branch of any milk-tree (*e. g.*, fig tree, &c.) in the south-west corner under the pandal, and offers cocoanuts and plantains to the Piḷḷaiyâr, and the bridegroom in his full-dress and orna-

ments plants the branch and seats himself on the Manavarei. The Guru utters some Mantras and finishes the ceremonies.

9. The bridegroom and the bride in grand procession go to the altar of their god, worship him and break cocoanuts. Having come home, they sit on the Manavarei facing the east with the bride on the bridegroom's left. The Thâli is put in a little wooden box, the Guru first blesses it and sends it round the assembly to get the blessing of the old men present. This done, the Guru receives the Thâli back, and approaching the Manavarei, orders the young couple to stand up, the bridegroom with his face towards the bride. The bridegroom now treads upon the bride's left foot with his right; a cloth is held between them for a veil: the bridegroom receives the Thâli from the Guru and puts it on the bride's neck from the other side of the veil; and his sister ties it round the bride's neck. Just at this time the drums are beaten and trumpets blown; the women standing round make a deafening shout.

10. In the presence of the whole assembly the bride's father comes forward and says, "I have given my daughter in marriage to M. N.'s son," this he says three times and pours water on the joined hands of the couple. After this they tie their hands with a colored handkerchief.

11. The bride and the bridegroom are then seated upon two stools, and their respective friends pour milk on their heads and give them sacred ashes, with which to besmear their foreheads, which they do.

12. When all these ceremonies have been completed the couple walk round the Manavarei three times and then retire into a room where the friends of the bridegroom sing adulatory songs. At night there is a procession of the young couple round the village in great pomp.

13. On the third day, a lighted candle is placed on the Manavarei, a Piḷḷaiyâr placed at the bottom of the lamp, and cocoanuts, plantains, betel and flowers offered to it with a measure full of uncooked rice. The bride then bathes and cooks some rice. The rice being ready, the bride and the bridegroom stand facing the east their friends take two dishes of the rice and wave them before the face of the couple and then throw a handful of rice behind them to avert the evil eye, the remainder of the cooked rice is given to the barber and the washerman.

14. A new plough is made by the carpenter, with which the bridegroom turns up the earth for about two or three yards around. The bride levels the earth, thus turned up and then sows some seed in it. The bride's brother pricks the bridegroom with an *ox goad,* and the bridegroom's sister fills up the holes, into which the bride had dropped the seed; while doing so, the bride asks the bridegroom's sister, "Why do you fill the holes that I made?" To this she replies, "If you give your daughter in marriage to my son, I will open them." Thus saying, she runs before the couple and makes a feint of preventing them entering the house. When asked to open, she answers, "Yes, if you promise to

give your daughter in marriage to my son." If her request is complied with, she opens the door and lets them in.

15. This is followed by a very unnecessary sort of farce :—Under the pandal four sticks are fixed so as to form a square, and a thread is passed round the four sticks ; by the side of each of the sticks is placed a pot ; one of which holds cunjee water, another saffron water, another sandal water, and another betel. The bride's sister pours some from each of the pots on the bridegroom's head, who ejects betel juice on her head in return.

MARRIAGE CEREMONIES
OF THE
REDDIES.

The Reddies like the Naickers, are obliged to marry their sisters' daughters, *i. e.*, their nieces. They have no fixed time for celebrating their marriages, but generally speaking, their marriages take place before the bride has attained the age of puberty : but having determined upon celebrating a marriage, an Astrologer is consulted, in order to ascertain a lucky day for the event ; and having ascertained it, a message is sent to the bride's friends desiring them to get all things ready.

2. They next procure ten or fifteen earthen pots, which are ornamented with lines drawn by particolored chalk upon the outer surface, and place them

in a convenient place, one over the other, the females of the house chanting in Telúgú.

3. A pandal, or shed, is next erected, and to chase away evil or malignant demons, a few branches of the Ficus religiosa, Dalbergia arborea, and the tamarind, are bound together and placed near to the door through which the guests will enter. All things being ready, and the auspicious day arrived, the bridegroom sets out in an open *palkee* for the residence of the bride; before doing which, however, he submits his head and chin to the barber's skill, for the first time in his life.

4. The operation over, the young Reddy, with his young men, approach the house, a loud blast of trumpets announcing their arrival: he descends from the palkee and enters the pandal, where, after a little time, the bride presents herself, taking her seat on his left. The usual salutations over, he ties round her *neck* the *Thâli* corresponding to our ring. The Thâli used by Reddies differs from those used by other classes of Hindùs, which are richly ornamented with gold. The Reddy uses a plain twisted cord of cotton thread, besmeared with saffron, and entirely devoid of ornament of any kind. They have a legend which accounts for this:—"In days of yore a Reddy chief was about to be married, and he accordingly sent for a goldsmith, and desiring him to make a splendid Thâli, gave him the price of it beforehand. The smith was a drunkard, and neglected his work: the day for the celebration of marriage arrived, but there was no Thâli; whereon the old chief, plucking a few threads from his garment, twisted them

into a cord, and tied it round the neck of the bride and this became a custom." The Thâli having been tied, she is married.

5. Chunam, saffron, and cotton-seed are next ground into a fine powder, to which a little water is added to give it the consistency of paste: a small portion of this is fixed between the eyes of the very near relatives of the young couple, in order to avert the "evil eye." The bridegroom, with his bride, are now conducted to the palkee, in order to be paraded round the village; the bride muffled up in her garments, so as to preclude the possibility of the sharpest eye in the throng, detecting the minutest portion of her visage. The friends of both parties throng round the palkee; the rear is occupied by the loungers of the village; a rustic band moves to the front; and all being ready, the cortége moves on, the musicians doing their best.

6. Having paraded the village, its guardian deities, as well as those of the cardinal points, are propitiated by offerings of fruit and flowers; and this ceremony ended, they return to the bride's house. The bridegroom, however, gets on horseback, and takes a ride through the place, attended by his young men, evidently pleased by the attentions shown him by the villagers. On this occasion the ten or fifteen pots beforementioned are carried in procession before him, and afterwards carefully laid by; an injury to any of them being said to forbode certain misfortune to the young couple.

7. At night again, both of them ascend the palkee,

and are conducted through the principal thoroughfares of the village. If the married couple are wealthy, this is conducted with great éclat, hundreds of lighted torches precede the procession, each individual, male and female, being supplied with one, at their own cost, so that the blaze of light almost makes the surrounding darkness visible. The procession at length passes beyond the village, and moves on about a furlong.

8. When it returns, the musicians announce it to those who remained behind by a blast from their trumpets. This midnight serenade is called "*entering the city,*" and is considered by the natives the grandest part of the ceremony.

N. B.—In this caste and also in the Naicker caste, Polygamy of the worst description is *legally* practised. It is no uncommon thing to meet a man married to two sisters, and having a family by each. I know an instance of a man having three sisters to wife at the same time.

MARRIAGE CEREMONIES

OF THE

IRLUVERS OR WEAVERS.

When a marriage has been determined upon, both parties seek an auspicious day, in which to determine the Parisam and to arrange other preliminaries in the presence of most of their nearest relations and friends.

Accordingly, on the day fixed, the bridegroom's relations go to the bride's house with a cloth for the bride, saffron and betel.

2. On their arrival they are hospitably entertained; after which the bride's party asks, whether all the nearest relations have come with them. This answered, the bridegroom's party then puts the same question and asks whether all their nearest relations are present. If they are not, they wait until they arrive. Only when there are ill-feelings among the families, are near relations absent on such an occasion, and in this caste many wait for this opportunity to display their hate and enmity, knowing that they will be most earnestly begged to honor the occasion with their presence.

3. The bridegroom's uncle asks the bride's uncle to settle the Parisam, who in reply wishes the other to commence the business, and he accordingly mentions the sum. The bride's uncle again asks, which sort of marriage the other would like, whether the one with palkee or the other without it. One of the two is chosen. If the one with palkee be chosen, the bridegroom's uncle ties sixteen little pieces of gold, worth each Rupees 2-1-4, in a white piece of cloth, and with the consent of all gives it to the bride's uncle together with a certain number of cocoanuts, plantains, betel and odoriferous stuffs, which he takes with the consent of all *his* relations and gives to the bride's father.

4. The bride bathes, puts on the new cloth brought, and is adorned with jewels, saffron and flowers. The Guru is called for, and he asks the names of the couple,

and upon the names he composes a doggerel verse, giving his opinion of the intended union; all which is written on an olei, hence called *Múhúrtha-paṭ-ṭólei.*

5. On the day appointed for celebrating the marriage, several of the bride's relations go to fetch the bridegroom, who is adorned with earrings and flowers, placed in a palkee and carried round his village in grand procession, after which he sets out for the bride's house. On his arrival the bride bathes and is adorned and taken round the village in a palkee; after which there is a feast for the relations of both parties.

6. Then the ceremonies of tying the Thâli follow:—At the request of the bridegroom's father, the Guru sits upon the Manavarei facing the north, and orders the bridegroom to adorn himself; who then shaves, bathes and comes before the Guru, by whose directions he fixes a branch of the fig tree in the south-west corner and seats himself on the Manavarei. The Guru then utters some Mantras which are repeated by the bridegroom after him.

7. The bride is also brought to the Manavarei, and the Guru repeats some Mantras to be repeated after him by her. The wedding cloths of both are then brought before the Guru who blesses them and returns them. Having put on their respective wedding cloths, they both come to the Manavarei and seat themselves facing the east.

8. The Thâli is then brought on a dish, over some betel and areca-nuts, and given to the Guru who blesses it, and at an auspicious moment gives it to the

bridegroom who holds it out *towards* the bride's neck, round which his sister ties it. This done, the bride's father comes forward, and the whole to assembly says "I have this day given my daughter to M. N.'s son in marriage, in the presence of this Brahmin our Guru, and you my relations and friends." This he says three times, and on each occasion pours water over their united hands. Just at this time, some one places twelve pieces of gold in the bridegroom's hands and pours water over them, and others give a small bundle of saffron and cotton seed and pour water on his hand. In some cases the bride's father makes a ring of pure gold and presents it to the bridegroom.

9. The chief men of the village make dots of cotton seed and saffron water on the bridegroom's forehead to avert the evil eye. The young couple then walk round the Manavarei three times and then retire to a room where there is prepared a kind of sweetmeat, of which the bride gives three times to the bridegroom, who eats it; and in return gives her of the same three times, and she eats it.

10. The next day both the bride and the bridegroom are seated facing the east; the bride's brother rubs oil on the bridegroom, and the bridegroom's sister rubs the bride. Then follows a feast for the relations of both parties.

MARRIAGE CEREMONIES

OF THE

KICOLARS.

On the appointed day the bridegroom's relations take with them cocoanuts, plantains, betel and a new cloth for the bride, and set out for her house where all her relations have previously assembled. The bride bathes and is adorned with flowers, saffron, sandal-wood powder and jewels, and the new cloth is put on her.

2. On a dish of betel the bridegroom's uncle places twenty-three pieces of gold and gives them to the bride's uncle who gives them to the bride's father. Betel is now served to all present. This is the "ceremony of confirmation."

3. A day or two before the marriage, the relations of the bride fetch the bridegroom who adorns himself, proceeds round his village in great pomp and then sets out for the village of the bride, where he is brought to some other house than the bride's for a while. The bride adorned, is taken on the same palkee round her village in procession.

4. In some room of the bride's house a square is drawn with chunam, and the bride is placed within it adorned with the new cloth, jewels, sandal, flowers, &c., and her maidens stand round and shout.

5. The bridegroom in his full dress comes before the Guru near the Manavarei and repeats some Mantras after him. The bride has also to repeat some after him.

After this they are both seated on the Manavarei facing the east. The Guru blesses the Thâli, repeating several Mantras, and gives it to the bridegroom who reaches it towards the bride's neck, but his sister ties it round it.

6. The bride's father comes forward, and placing his daughter's hand in the bridegroom's, says three times, "this is your own;" upon which, he pours water on their united hands. Then they both walk round the Manavarei three times and retire.

7. In the morning of the next day, both of them are seated on the Manavarei; oil is brought in two little cups:—of these the bride's brother takes one and rubs oil on the bridegreom, while the bridegroom's sister takes the other and rubs oil on the bride. They then seat themselves on the Manavarei.

8. The bride's father brings a plateful of small cakes, cocoanuts and plantains, and over these he places ten Rupees or twenty; the whole he sets before the bridegroom who asks leave of his father and relations to touch the plate. If they give permission, he touches it; and his sisters then take it away, eat the cakes, &c., and give the money to their parents.

9. If a father is able to give his daughter dowry, the bride and the bridegroom are placed on the Manavarei facing the east. All the relations are present; and in their presence he gives them whatever he is able; and in return the bridegroom's father bears a portion of the marriage expenses, either a third or half portion falls to him.

MARRIAGE CEREMONIES

OF THE

KOLIAR PULLARS.

There are seven tribes or classes in this caste, and no man of the caste is allowed to take him a wife from his own tribe or class, because the women of his class are considered his sisters.

2. A marriage is first determined upon privately among the parents of both the bridegroom and the bride. On an auspicious day both the parties meet in the bride's house, and the bridegroom's relations inform the people of the village where the bride lives, of the intended marriage, and request them to come in the evening to the bride's house. Accordingly, all the men of the village meet in the bride's house. The uncles of both the bridegroom and the bride must be present on the occasion, as without them a marriage cannot be arranged.

3. Betel bought by both parties is then placed before the chief man who is called the *Kûdûmban* or "*Ambalakarun,*" and he appoints two young men to distribute them to the people assembled. This being done, the *Kûdûmban* asks the bridegroom's father the reason for inviting the village people. He then states that he has come to arrange a marriage between his son and the daughter of their host, and ends by requesting that his wishes may be complied with. The Kûdûmban then asks the bride's father if

he is willing to give his daughter, and if a favorable answer is returned he asks both parties whether they are going to have a "*pandal-marriage*" or "*kúlavi-marriage*," (*kúlavi* means a "shout" of joy). Pandal-marriage is attended with ceremonies and pomps, the other is a plain marriage. The parties choose either the one or the other. The Múhúrtha day is then fixed; and the people having partaken of refreshment, disperse.

4. On the Múhúrtha day, the bride's father requests the village men to help him in constructing a pandal. (It is not necessary to have a pandal in the bridegroom's house.) They all meet in the middle of the day, and after constructing the pandal, sit on mats spread under it. Betel is placed before the Kûdûmban who orders two young men to distribute it. Each man should receive five nuts and half a *pollam** of betel.

5. This being done, Parisam is then given as follows:—the Kûdûmban sends for a brass plate and a stool with three legs. The bride's uncle sits on the northern side, the bridegroom's uncle on the southern side, and the stool is placed in the middle with the plate upon it. The Parisam is twenty-two Rupees, which should all be changed into two-anna silver pieces. The bridegroom's uncle mixes these annas with paddy and pours them by his right hand (supported by his left) into the vessel. The bridegroom's

* A pollam is equal to oz. 1, dr. 3·75.

uncle, by the permission of the Kûdûmban, takes them and ties them in his cloth.

6. If the bridegroom belongs to another village, the Parisam is "poured out" after his arrival. The bridegroom first leaves his village with a show of pomp, and when he arrives near the bride's village he alights and remains outside the village for a little time and then sends word to the Kûdûmban of the place, who, with the village men, comes out to meet the bridegroom with trumpets and drums, and conducting him into the village, places him in a friend's house. Early in the morning, the Kûdûmban and the village people meet in the bride's house and invite the bridegroom through a cousin of his. He is received with joy and shoutings, and is seated under the pandal. Betel is distributed, a string of golden beads is tied round his neck; and he is then placed on a horse and led to a well or a tank to bathe himself. On the way, a chuckler holds an umbrella over the bridegroom. After washing he dresses himself with his best cloths and returns to the bride's house with drums beating. Two young men spread a white cloth in the pandal, on which he throws cotton seeds mixed with grass which are given to him by his uncle, and walks round a post three times, and a pot containing fire is placed in the centre of the pandal. This done, he is again sent to the house where he first stayed.

7. The bride comes out from the house to the pandal with a piece of colored rope tied round one of her hands, and is placed on horseback together with one

of her cousins who covers her head with his own cloth, and is taken to a well or a tank, where she performs all the ceremonies which the bridegroom had before gone through, and is then allowed to return to the house.

8. The bridegroom is then sent for, and entering at the middle of the pandal, is dressed with a handsome pair of new cloths and garlands are put on his neck: the bride then comes out handsomely dressed and stands near him. (Up to this time, the bridegroom and the bride are kept separate from each other). The bridegroom's sister now ties the *Thâli* for him.

9. The bride is taken again into the house, and the bridegroom goes out for a ride attended with shoutings and drums, along the streets of the village. When he comes back close to the house, the bride's father with others go out to meet him with garlands and sandal powder; and all enter the pandal where the bridegroom is seated on a piece of a wood, covered with white cloth, his sister on his left side. The bride then comes out, and is made to recline on the bosom of the bridegroom's sister. The Kûdûmban then takes the right hand of the bride and causes the bridegroom to take hold of it by his right hand. The bride's father comes next with a cup of water and pours it on their hands, saying these words:—"Oh people! I now pour water publicly on the hand of A., the son of B., and that of C., my daughter." If a rich man, he also mentions the dowry which he intends to give. Both the bridegroom and the bride having their hands in the same

position walk round a post and the fire-pot already placed there, and then retire into the house, where they sit on a colored mat. The garlands are next taken off the bridegroom's neck and put on the neck of the bride. A colored box with some cocoanuts, betel and rice are placed before them. Out of this, the Kûdûmban takes one cocoanut, seven areca-nuts and fourteen betel leaves, and putting them in a vessel, gives them to the bride. She stands up, receives them, and giving them to the bridegroom, worships him, putting her hands on her head. She then sits down. The Kûdûmban receives back the cocoanut and dividing it into two pieces, gives the *female piece* of it *i. e.*, the piece which has the hole, to the bride, and the *male piece, i. e.*, the piece having no hole in it, to the bridegroom. He again takes them back from their hands and cuts the kernel which together with four areca-nuts, and seven betel leaves are given to the bridegroom ; and five pieces of the kernel together with three areca-nuts and seven betel leaves are given to the bride.

10. Then follows the feast which continues for three days. On the third day, the string of golden beads is taken off the bridegroom's neck. On the fourth day the bridegroom returns to his house with the bride.

MARRIAGE CEREMONIES

OF THE

CHUCKLERS.

When about to arrange a marriage, the bridegroom's party take a bottle of arrack to the intended bride's house and give it to her father to drink. If he consents to the proposed marriage, he gives another bottle of arrack in return to the bridegroom's father to drink; and then an Astrologer is consulted for his opinion as to a propitious day both for Parisam and for the intended marriage.

2. A Parisam of six and a quarter Rupees, one kottah of chōlum, five measures of rice and some oil with saffron and cocoanuts should be taken to the bride's house, together with a string of beads and an ōlei for the ears. The bridegroom's sister should carry some of these on her head. The string of beads is then tied by the bridegroom's sister to the bride's neck. This is their *Thâli*. From this day she is considered as his wife. Then for five fanams taken out of the Parisam, arrack and other spirits are bought. Both parties drink deeply of these spirits.

3. On the Múgúrtha day, a vessel full of milk is brought, and all the relations of the bridegroom take handfuls of it and pour it on the bridegroom's head, and which his friend rubs well on him. After he bathes, he is taken outside the village to a place where there is an *Auverei* plant ("Cassia Auriculata.") Three little sticks are posted so as to form a triangle, and a potful

of rice is cooked between the three sticks, which are supposed to represent a little hut. The bridegroom and his relations partake of the food.

4. The bridegroom then starts for the residence of the bride; but stays somewhere outside the village; while the bride bathes in milk as he did. The bride is then taken outside the village where the bridegroom is waiting, and there, at the side of an Auverei, they post two sets of three sticks as a hut for each of them, and there they cook food. Their respective uncles take a handful of rice, bring it round their heads and throw it behind them to avert the evil eye. The remaining rice is eaten by the entire company, with the bride and the bridegroom.

5. The bride is taken round the huts three times by her uncle, who also places her right hand in the bridegroom's left.

6. Then both the bridegroom and the bride are taken to the house of the bride. While coming, the bridegroom's sisters wave the lighted camphor to the bride and receive money from her father or brothers.

7. Then in the front of the house the bridegroom sits on a stool with a cloth on it, and the bride pours water on him. The bride then puts on the same cloth and sits down, and the bridegroom pours water on her, and thus both bathe.

8. In the same places the bridegroom makes a plough of two sticks and ploughs the ground wet by the water in which they bathed, and the bride takes

conjee to him in a pot. She also takes a little child with her, which she gives to the bridegroom who kisses it and returns it. After this two or three rings are cast in into a pot of water, and they both are made to take them out with a view to ascertain which of them will in future have power over the other.

9. Then they both are taken into the house; while entering they dip their hands near the door-posts inside into a salt pot by way of amusement, and the bridegroom's relations beat the bride by way of a joke.

10. The marriages of this caste are conducted with brawling and noise, owing to the quantity of spirits consumed on the occasion; and they do not hesitate to divorce each other even for trifles. I have known a man of this caste to be married three times to different women during a single year.

KARÚMÁNTHARUM
OR
FUNERAL CEREMONY.

Karumantharum derived from two Sanscrit words *Karuma,* "deed," and *Antara,* "last," is generally performed on a specific day ordained by the Hindu Sastras. The Vîshnuvites and the Saivites observe it on the sixteenth day; the Kshatriyas on the fourteenth; the Vaisyas on the fifteenth; and the Brahmins on the twelfth day after the decease of the individual.

This ceremony consists in going through several processes or rites, each of which is calculated to accomplish only a certain peculiar portion of the whole ceremony.

Although there exists a considerable degree of dissimilarity in the method in which these several rites are performed by the various sects, yet, their motives seem all to agree, in an essential point, viz: the salvation of the soul of the deceased.

Among these several rites, the most important are:—

1. *Sutravesarchanum* from two Sanscrit words meaning "thread" and "to divest." This rite is performed on the fifteenth night, at home, for the wife of the deceased, preparatory to the sixteenth day's ceremony or Karumantharum. Her connexions and friends assemble and adorn her with flowers and the best cloths and jewelry in her possession; this done, they place her in a

particular spot and weep for awhile, embrace her and then pull their hair, beat the ground with their feet and beat their breasts. After this, she is divested of all her ornaments and deserted by all the females of the family except the widows, who alone are expected to perform the remainder of the ceremony; these women, who like her, are widows, after sympathizing with, and consoling her, take her into a room set apart for the purpose (where a mat has been placed with a pillow upon it; a light considered sacred, a potful of cow's milk, together with some paddy and salt in a tray) and causing her to sit on this mat; one of them unties the Thâli, worn on the neck, and throws it into the milk-pot. She is next caused to lie prostrate on the mat with her head towards the light, and then covering her all over with a new cloth, one takes the salt and paddy, and gives a little to each of the women who had retired, as an indication of their having discharged their duty; who then re-entering the room, first throw the salt over the recently made widow (her face is now uncovered) and then throw the paddy over the light, worship it, and again leave the apartment. While the widow continues in this position, each of her connexions and friends present her with a new cloth, depositing it near her head.

2. *Vapana-karumum*, from two sanscrit words *Vapana*, "shaving;" and *karuma*, "deed." The following morning, the sixteenth day, at about five o'clock A. M., "the lighter of the pile" or the *Kurtha*, goes with his connexions and friends to the neighbourhood of a tank. Here, he and his nearest connexions have their heads and mustachios shaved; then washing themselves in the

tank, the Kurtha alone ties a piece of muslin round his waist and puts the two marks on his forehead, indicative of mourning.

This done, the priest and others assemble at a little distance from the tank, and the Kurtha boils some rice for a "meat-offering" called Pôngal.

3. *Antyeshti*, signifying a ceremony performed for the benefit of the dead. The priest makes a figure representing the deceased, of the sacred grass called (*Agrostis linearis*, or) cúsa (*Poa cynosuroides*) and placing it on a bier, gives it to the Kurtha, putting at the same time the sacred thread called *Púnúl*, across his shoulder, and a ring called *Pavitra* made of cúsa grass, on his finger. The Kurtha carries and places the figure in the south-east corner of the *pandal** in the part called *Agni-mooly* (from *Agni*, "fire;" and *Mooly*, "a corner)" the corner occupied by the god of fire. Then the priest taking a seat at the western side of a hole,† draws five figures resembling the lotus flower, with five differently colored chalks, around the mouth of the pit, and places four earthern vessels on the four corners, having a piece of sacred thread tied round their necks. This done, he fills them with mango leaves and places tender cocoanuts on their mouths, making four dots, with rice mixed with ground saffron and sandalwood, on the four sides of each of them. Then setting a plantain tree against each of the poles, already set up on the

---

* A Shed constructed a few yards from the tank.

† About 2½ feet square and 1½ feet in depth, sunk in the centre of the pandal with four poles set on its corners.

four corners of the hole, he adorns them by tying strings of mango leaves from the extremity of one pole to that of another. He then makes a fire in the hole and pours ghee and boiled rice upon it, and extinguishes it with cow's milk; this he does alternately, for about an hour, repeating certain incantations followed up by the other Brahmins around him. Afterwards he takes the figure left in the Agni-mooly, and as if by the influence of his priestly office, transfering to the image, the sins of the deceased, burns it to ashes, which he carries and throws into the tank; thereby implying the absolution of the soul of the deceased.

4. *Nugna serarthum* from two Sanscrit words *Nugna*, "naked;" and *S'raddha*, "to give with love." This rite consists in presenting to a Brahmin a black blanket, a pair of sandals, a pair of new cloths, rice, ghee, pulse, and vegetables, together with some money; who makes amends for the incongruities that might have crept in during the performance of the rites already observed, by atoning for the sin of the Kurtha consequent thereon. This Brahmin, as soon as he has received the presents, turns away, and avoids the presence of the Kurtha for one day, because it is believed, that, should he see him before this period expires, his attempt at atonement becomes ineffectual.

5. *S'ila-abishekam* from two Sanscrit words *S'ila*, "a stone," and *Ab'hisheka*, "anointing." This rite is performed as follows:—The *Pani-seivône* or the "person who announces" the ceremony to the public, procures three *S'ilas* or stones of a conical shape, and delivers them to

the *Purôhita* or the "Calendar Brahmin," who, setting them in a brass tray, gives them to the Kurtha who anoints them with sesamum oil, which act is called *Tailôthagum* from two Sanscrit words *Taila*, "oil," and *Udaka*, "water;" and washing them, anoints them again with curds, milk, ghee, lime-juice, cocoanut water and honey, and washes them again. Then he wraps each of them together with a piece of the cúsa grass in a small piece of linen, their extremities however being visible and upon which are traced as many marks as the Kurtha himself wears on his forehead, and this act is called *Vastrôthagum* from the Sanscrit *Vastra*, "cloth," and *Udaka*, "water." He then presents nine Brahmins, each with a pair of new cloths, rice, ghee, pulse and vegetables, together with some honey which is called *Nava-serarthum* from *Navan*, "nine," and *S'raddha*, "to give with love;" and these are given in the name of his three ancestors, his father, grandfather and great-grandfather, whom the three stones set up are intended symbolically to represent.

6. *S'ilasthapanum* from *S'ila*, "stone," and *Stapana*, "to place." The Kurtha spreading a plantain leaf under the pandal and scattering some rice upon it, removes the S'ilas from the brass tray and places them upon the leaf, then he erects a small shed over them, with a tender cocoanut leaf, in the shape of an arch, and placing two tender cocoanuts, with two cocoanut shoots in its sides, adorns it with flowers. This done, a service is first offered to the S'ilas by the Kurtha repeating an incantation after the Purôhita; then an oblation is

offered to them, of broken cocoanuts, plantains, sweetmeats, some Bengal gram, beaten rice and betel-nut, together with the rice before prepared for a "meat-offering." At the conclusion of this rite, *ten Brahmins* are presented each with a peculiar kind of present: to one is given a cow with its calf, and called *Gô-da'num;* and to another, a piece of land is given, which is called *Bhoo-da'num;* and to the third, a half measure of oil seeds with some money called *Tailô-da'num;* to the fourth, some gold, called *Hiran'ya-da'num;* to the fifth, some ghee and money called *Ab'hya-da'num;* to the sixth, a pair of cloths with some money, called *Vastrô-da'num;* to the seventh, some raw rice, called *Dhanya-da'num*; to the eighth, some jaggery, called *Guda-da'num;* to the ninth, a black blanket, called *Rawpea-danum;* and to the tenth, some salt, called *Lava'na-da'num.* These ten Brahmins are, by means of their several influences, conjointly to contribute to the tranquil migration of the soul to its first station in the divine regions.* This done, the Kurtha and his connexions each putting upon the stones, a handful of raw rice, called *Vaikarisee,* from two Tamil words, *Vai,* "mouth;" and *Arisee,* "rice;" the *Paniseivone* blows

* The departed soul does not become entitled to admission into heaven until three of its progenies are dead—the son, grandson, and the great grandson. Until then, it has to go through three intermediate stations. The incumbent of the highest is titled *Ahtheeta;* and that of the second, *Rudra;* and that of the lowest or first, *Vásu.* Thus adoption becomes so absolutely necessary in cases where a Hindu is without male issue.

the sacred chank, to deter evil spirits from intercepting the progress of the soul towards its destination.

7. *S'ilayuttavusanum* (*S'ila,* "stone;" *Utta,* "to take;" and *Asana,* "seat,") the S'ilas are carried by one of the connexions of the Kurtha in a tray and placed on his shoulders as he sit sat the east gate of the pandal opposite to the tank; who surrounded by all the assembly, carries them down to the tank and gradually descending into it, causes them to be washed away from the tray, which act is especially called *S'ila-gunga-nēckapanum* from *S'ila,* "stone;" *Gūnga,* "water;" and *nēchapanum,* "to leave." After which, the Kurtha washing himself, the whole of the assembly doing likewise, leaves the sacred thread and the ring put on him by the priest, in the tank, and wraps himself with his usual cloths, putting on his usual marks on the forehead.

Punniaga vajanum, from three Sancrit words *Pun'ya,* "purity;" *Aga,* "to tell;" and *Vachana,* "a word;" is performed as follows:—A plantain leaf being laid in the centre of the pandal with some raw rice spread on it, the priest making a representation of the god Piḷḷaiyâr, and placing it on one side of the leaf, on which a circle is then described, he places a brass pot within it, filled with water and mango leaves, having a cocoanut on its mouth; after which, he makes four dots on the four sides of the brass pot, with rice mixed with powdered saffron and sandalwood, and adorns it and the Piḷḷaiyâr with flowers. He then offers some incense to them with incantations, and then an oblation consisting of broken cocoanuts, fruits, betel-nuts, &c., accompanied with incantations. This done, the priest sanctifies the Kurtha (who is in a polluted state from the time he had set fire to the pile) and the places trodden by him under the pandal. Then follows *Ekangum* from *Eka*, "one;" and *Anga*, "body;" which consists in the giving of certain gifts to a Brahmin; namely, an elephant, a sheep, a cap, a bag to keep his sacred ashes in, a *cadjan* fan, a stool, a pair of sandals, a basket, rice, ghee and vegetables, together with some money, who is then supposed to transfer the sins of the deceased to himself, and consequently, having received the above gifts he turns away from the presence of the donor, or Kurtha, and for twenty-one days avoids seeing him as well as the locality which he inhabits.

This is followed by another called *Shoḍashan*, signifying sixteen, which consists in the giving of gifts to sixteen Brahmins. Strictly speaking, according to Sastra, this rite ought to be repeated monthly, besides quarterly, for the space of one year; and on each of these occasions, one of the sixteen Brahmins is presented with a pair of new cloths, rice, pulse, vegetables, curds, ghee, a ball of tamarind, together with money, for the support of the departed soul, during its migration to its destination, which occupies a period of twelve months or one divine day. But it is generally performed with the other rites of the Karúmántharum, lest the Kurtha should by accident or otherwise be precluded from accomplishing it in accordance to Sastra, and consequently not only distress the departed soul, but bring on himself a curse.

8. *Sapta-kurnam, Sapta* signifying "seven;" and *Kurnam* "to join;" is performed by the *Purôhita*, who mixing raw rice, milk, honey, curds, cow's urine, ghee and oil seeds together, to form a mass, places it upon a tray with a few pieces of the cùsa grass and then divides it into three portions, intended symbolically to represent three of the ancestors of the deceased, who are in the intermediate divine regions—Atheetas. Thus the deceased becomes assimilated with his ancestors with respect to their divinity, and entitled to admission into the lowest or last station in the divine region, occupied by his father, or Vasu, who succeeds his father, or Rudra, who fills Atheeta's stations vacated for heaven. This done, seven Brahmins are presented each with a pair of new cloths, rice, a ball of tamarind, ghee and pulse, as marks of gratitude for the above promotions.

Lastly, *Svarga-pathum* from *Swarga*, "heaven;" and *pada*, "road;" which is performed by presenting a Brahmin with a pair of new cloths, rice, ghee, pulse and vegetables together with some money, whereby the great-grandfather of the deceased is supported during his progress to heaven.

In conclusion, the Kurtha and the whole of the attendants assemble and dine in one of the Brahmins' houses in the neighbourhood of the tank (who being informed in the morning, has a repast prepared for as many as are expected). Besides them several others, to whom it was not convenient to be present at the ceremony, meet here, and partake of this solemn feast. After which they return again to the pandal; when most of the connexions of the Kurtha then assembled, present him with cloths, which passed through the hands of the *Purôhita* consecrated and attended with blessings. This done, the assembly being served out with betel-nuts, &c., quit the place for home accompanied by music. On their way, they perform a service at the very first Piḷḷaiyâr kôvil (temple) or Pagôda they meet with. No sooner they arrive at the house of the deceased than they first worship the sacred light which was lighted, the night the widow was divested of her Thâli. After which, being again served with betel-nuts, &c., they condole with the widow and Kurtha and then disperse.

THE END.